Linguistics
and Foreign Language
Teaching

Linguistics and Foreign Language Teaching

Denis Girard

Translated and Edited by R. A. Close

Longman

LONGMAN GROUP LIMITED
London

*Associate companies, branches and representatives
throughout the world*

© Longman Group Limited 1972

First published 1972

ISBN 0 582 52603 5

Printed by St. Pauls Press Ltd, Malta

CONTENTS

GENERAL INTRODUCTION

The Author and his Work

To many who will read this book, Denis Girard needs no introduction. Well-known on both sides of the Atlantic, he has for several years been prominent at international meetings on foreign language teaching, and particularly at conferences under the auspices of the Council of Europe. As Deputy Director, then Director of B.E.L.C., the *Bureau pour l'Enseignement de la Langue et de la Civilisation française à l'Etranger* (Bureau for the teaching of French language and civilisation abroad), he was in a key position from which to influence the teaching of French as a foreign language. Now, as Regional Inspector for the *Académie* (educational zone) *de Paris*, with special responsibilities for English, he is the inspiration behind much of the modern teaching of English in France. At one time, he conducted a highly successful experiment in teaching English in Morocco; and his account of it (in *Les Langues Modernes*, September-October 1962) is the basis of some of the ideas developed in this book. He gave the opening lecture at the Conference of the International Association of Teachers of English as a Foreign Language in January 1970; and in April of that year the paper he presented at the Institute of Linguists' Conference on 'English – a European Language?' was outstanding. Many who have not had the opportunity of hearing his lucid and stimulating talks, will know him as a former Cultural Attaché at the French Embassy in London, or as one of the compilers of Cassell's *New French Dictionary* (1961) and of Cassell's *Compact French-English/English-French Dictionary*, or as a leading spirit in the team that produced *Passport to English*, which is becoming used as a textbook for the study of English as a foreign language in France and in other countries as well.

The twentieth century, since its beginning, has seen two major developments in the field of language. One has been the increasing study of foreign languages as an integral part of general education; the other, the astonishing growth of the science of linguistics. The two have reacted on each other. Teachers of foreign languages, proceeding empirically and by their intuition, found themselves dealing in a practical way with many problems which linguists have later investigated and have often been able to elucidate. Linguists in their turn have revealed facts, formulated scientific statements and evolved fundamental theories, which have profoundly influenced language teaching.

The French-speaking world has been very much concerned with and in these developments. As Girard will explain, we owe much of the inspiration of modern linguistics to Ferdinand de Saussure. Works on linguistics are very much in evidence in Paris bookshops today. With regard to the teaching of foreign languages, the teaching of French and the maintenance of it as a world language have been throughout the century a matter of deep concern to the French nation as a whole. Indications of that are the very efficient French Institutes to be found in many of the world's cities, and the title of the Journal *Le Français dans le Monde.* At the same time, over three million young people in France are now studying English, as well as senior academics and businessmen who realise that English is indispensable as a *lingua franca* in international relations.

The author of this book, as we have seen, has played a prominent part in more than one aspect of this intense linguistic activity in France. He is first and foremost a teacher, and he speaks and writes as an experienced member of the language teaching profession. Like many people in this modern age and as a typical son of France, he seeks a theoretical and reasoned justification for what he is doing. In any teaching, to think out clearly what one is doing, to believe firmly in it, and to maintain continuity in the method one chooses, is more than half the battle. In language teaching, the centuries-old foundation of logical grammar, inherited from the study of Latin and Greek, has collapsed. It is disconcerting to many serious educationists to find that the new foundations which modern linguistics provides are, too often, liable to shift. Linguistic theories are evolving so rapidly that by the time a new book on the subject has finally emerged from the publishers it is said to be already out of date. That is no doubt inevitable in any rapidly developing science. But language teaching in the average school classroom, involved as it is with the planning and administration of national education; in many countries with the compilation and approval of official syllabuses; with the preparation and publication of textbooks; and above all with the mysterious process of learning during childhood, cannot rest on foundations that undergo upheaval year by year. In any case, as Denis

Girard points out, the aims of linguistics and of language teaching are different. Language teaching must be free to take from linguistics what suits its purpose best; and it is not dependent on linguists alone. Girard's strong plea that language teaching should establish itself as an independent discipline is timely and will be warmly welcomed by educationists who have felt bewildered every time their underlying theories are turned upside down.

Girard has himself anticipated criticism of his book that might arise in certain circles. He has found the notion of *structure* a very fertile one in language teaching. It still is fertile in that subject, as in others, including linguistics. In his lecture to the Association of Teachers of English as a Foreign Language in 1970, he spoke with some impatience of those who now condemned "the abhorred sect of structuralists who had the great misfortune of being born and accomplishing their work in the pre-transformational grammar era, that is in the dark middle-ages of linguistics". He went on to say, "I have nothing against transformational-generative grammar. On the contrary, I firmly believe that this new approach to language analysis has given a new impetus to linguistic research and I see no reason why language teaching should not eventually benefit from it, as it has from structuralism". He also believes that truth may be found somewhere between two extremes; and that language teaching should be free to make use of a linguistic theory if it proves to be of practical help and even if it is no longer in fashion with leading linguists themselves.

Just as there has been — or should one say 'Just as there *was* during the 1960s?' — a swing against structuralism, so there has been — or was — a reaction against the ideas that language is primarily speech and that in using a language we tend to form patterns of behaviour. These notions, too, have been, and still are, of great importance to language teaching, and especially in countries, France and others, where full proficiency in the use of a foreign language has been frustrated by excessive attention to written, literary texts and to cerebral exercises, to the detriment of aural comprehension and spontaneous or quasi-spontaneous oral expression. The linguistics of the 1970s is already showing signs of reacting against the theories of the last decade. "At present," Noam Chomsky wrote in 1968, "the field is in considerable ferment, and it will probably be some time before the dust begins to settle and a number of issues are even tentatively resolved". Denis Girard believes that language didactics should keep at a distance — a respectful distance, by all means — from that ferment. Being in daily contact with teachers and pupils in school, he is well aware that while we are waiting for the dust to settle, classes are restive and teachers must know what they are expected to do. His sympathies are with the students and the teachers, even when he is leading the latter — in a way they will understand — 'towards a scientific conception' of their task.

Emphasis on a 'scientific conception', especially in the planning, construction and use of language textbooks, is laid throughout these pages. It was repeated in Girard's address to the Association of Teachers of English as a Foreign Language in 1970 when he quoted the prophecy made fifty years ago by H. E. Palmer in the following passage:

> "If we asked a hundred different language teachers to design what each considered an ideal course or textbook, the result at the present day would certainly be a hundred different courses . . . it would prove that few or no fundamental principles are generally recognised. If, however, at some date in the distant future we were to make the same request, restricting our invitation to those who will have made a special study of the subject . . . we should probably find no great degree of diversity in the treatment; we should see the converging tendency at work, and should gather that the fundamental principles were beginning to stand out and to be respected".[1]

This book was basically a collection of articles, which were themselves scripts of lectures delivered to meetings of language teaching specialists. In editing the articles into book form and for an English-reading public, I have made certain internal re-arrangements to reduce overlap and supply references from one chapter to another. As links in the chain, I have written short introductions to each chapter. I have translated into English most of the examples used in the French version, partly for the benefit of teachers whose French is inadequate but mainly to help prove the author's point that methods and techniques which are valid for French will apply to other languages, such as English, as well.

R . A . C .

Highgate, February 1971

The Author's Preface

This book originated in a collection of articles on the teaching of foreign languages and particularly on the teaching of French. They were written during the last five or six years, at a time when the author occupied the posts of Deputy Director, then of Director of B.E.L.C. — *Bureau pour l'Enseignement de la Langue et de la Civilisation française à l'Etranger*. With one or two exceptions, they were all compiled from notes prepared for talks given at teacher-training courses or at language teaching conferences. That will explain their rather conversational style, which I have preferred to leave unchanged, in the hope that they will retain some of their spontaneity. Perhaps I might claim that the ideas expressed in them were forged in the fire of active service. For that reason, they may be less thoroughly worked out than the ideas we develop in the quiet of our study in writing a book or a paper intended primarily for publication. However, the various audiences who have heard the lectures from which this book started have expressed a wish to see them in print.

That is my excuse for assembling what I consider, rightly or wrongly, to be the most important of those scripts. The issues of the journals in which they first appeared have been exhausted, and so have such off-prints as were at one time available. I am not presuming that what I may have said and written about language teaching must at all costs be saved from oblivion. But I know too well that teachers who sincerely wish to keep abreast of new trends often feel the need for information in a condensed form and are on the look-out for anything that can help them in their everyday work.

That is what these articles are trying to provide. Their aim is, above all, a practical one. They are addressed to the practitioner in language-teaching, giving him the minimum of basic theory, without which no application is really valid. But they mainly concentrate on the manifold problems which arise when one starts applying theories in the classroom; and some of the articles were actually followed at the time by practical classroom demonstration.

The title I have chosen for the introductory chapter is a reflection of a double interest: 'Applied Linguistics' is a reference to the linguistic sources from which I have constantly drawn, explicitly or otherwise; while 'Language Didactics' implies a form of linguistic pedagogy which reconciles scientific theory with actual practice.

When I refer to 'language' it is to languages in general and not only to French as a foreign tongue. True, most of my examples were taken from French; and I would be the last to deny that each language presents its own problems in teaching. However, I believe that from the point of view of methodology and pedagogy, theories that are valid for French are also applicable to other languages.

This book no doubt has the inevitable defect of a composite publication: it does not follow a strict line of argument from one chapter to the next. I have, however, tried to present its various parts in some kind of logical sequence. Although the whole collection is concerned with linguistic pedagogy, I have arranged everything on the subject of Methodology in Part One. Part Two is concerned with Pedagogy, that is to say with how the lesson in the classroom can be planned and conducted. Part Three deals with the very important question of the Training and Further Training of Language Teachers. The introductory chapter was written especially for this book: it aims at explaining exactly what we mean by 'linguistics applied to language teaching'. The Conclusion looks to the future, and is based on a fairly detailed account of W. F. Mackey's *Language Teaching Analysis*.[1] I have given that chapter the title 'Towards a Scientific Conception of Language Teaching', because Professor Mackey really seems to have opened the way towards an original and fruitful form of 'Language Didactics' that can profit from the sciences to which it is indebted, while establishing its freedom to determine its own aims and its own procedures.

I am glad to be able to take this opportunity of thanking the editors of *Le Français dans le Monde* and of *Les Langues Modernes*, and the publishing houses of Hachette, Larousse, Didier and the Oxford University Press, for granting permission to reproduce the articles which now appear in this volume.

D. G.

Paris, 1970

Chapter 1

Applied Linguistics or Language Didactics?

In this introductory chapter, Denis Girard begins by considering the difficulties that beset the modern language teacher in the classroom, and draws attention to the all-important question of method. He then shows how ideas of language teaching method have been radically changed by the rapid advance of science in general, and by the development of linguistics and psychology in particular. He discusses the problem of applying those two sciences, linguistics especially, to the practical task of teaching, at a time when their fundamental theories are constantly evolving and are sometimes contradictory. His conclusion is not that we should return to language teaching as an 'art' free from any form of scientific control, but that we should develop it as a discipline in its own right, selecting from linguistics, psychology and other sources as well, whatever suits our professional purposes best. Rather than call that independent discipline a branch of applied linguistics, he prefers W. F. Mackey's term 'language didactics'. At least, it is a discipline with such a name that he proposes to deal with in this book.

WHY TEACHING A FOREIGN LANGUAGE IS DIFFICULT

The foreign language teacher is at a serious disadvantage compared with colleagues who teach the mother tongue. He works under a four-fold handicap:

First, he is usually given a very limited time-table. As against the ten or twelve hours a day when every child has the chance of practising his own tongue, the foreign language teacher has the problem of forming and developing a whole new set of linguistic habits in usually three or four hours a week of class instruction. In that respect alone, the odds are stacked against him.

A second obstacle is that, for the most part, his pupils lack any real motivation, once the novelty of the subject has worn off. In too many secondary schools, there seems to be no reason for learning a foreign language at all, except that it happens to be in the curriculum. As for the choice of language studied, a large-scale sociological survey would have to be carried out, country by country, before one could see what the various criteria are that decide the selection. No one will of course deny that we learn best what we want to learn. That is no doubt one of the reasons why we generally obtain the best results with adult students who have some compelling need to learn a foreign language, for professional purposes particularly. Motivation, plus the time-table factor, also accounts for the comparative ease with which the young child learns his own language, however difficult it is supposed to be and however backward he may be in his school-work.

The third difficulty, in many countries, is due to the fact that foreign language learning begins at the age of eleven or twelve — that is to say at the end, according to psychologists, of that very favourable period in a child's life when his powers of imitation are at their peak.

Last, and certainly not least, when we start teaching a foreign language we find ourselves fighting against the linguistic habits of the mother tongue which have by now been firmly entrenched. Our biggest problem will therefore be how to break down habits of hearing and producing speech, even to alter fixed ways of thought, and to establish new systems in their place. In other words, we have to start teaching a foreign language when what is called 'interference' by the mother tongue has become a positive hindrance.

Despite these difficulties, we are much more ambitious than our forebears. Modern means of communication, the vogue for travel and international exchanges, have made us regard a good command of the spoken language, not merely of the written, as indispensable. We go so far as to hope that we can reach results in a foreign language comparable with those we achieve in our own, notwithstanding the disparity in the circumstances under which we learn the one and the other.

Is there a way of overcoming those obstacles, of reaching that objective, in a reasonable time? Let us admit at once that there is no magic formula, but consider for a moment what in fact we can do to get over our difficulties.

THREE BASIC FACTORS

In every teaching situation, there are three basic factors: the pupil; the teacher; and the method, including the material taught. Success depends very largely on how suitable the method is for the teacher and on how well the teacher can adapt himself to the pupil.

The pupil is what he is, and we must accept him as he is. As such, he comes to class, apt or not so apt, with interests more or less awakened, with a certain capacity for attention and assimilation. We can no doubt take advantage of his interests, in a constant endeavour to compensate for his lack of motivation. However, we cannot expect too much: all we can do — and it is quite a lot — is to stimulate the process of learning that is at work in him already.

The teacher, on the other hand, has been prepared for his formidable task. But has he had the proper training? That raises a question which we shall come to in the third part of this book: how best to train the language teacher and improve his proficiency. We assume that he can be better equipped during his training years by being given special courses in linguistics, psychology and pedagogics. But in an age when every science and technique is changing so quickly, we can no longer assume that he can learn all he needs, once and for all, as a university student. The teacher, like the engineer, must always be bringing his knowledge and skill up to date. It may well be necessary one day to put Gaston Berger's[1] idea of perpetual training into practice.

The third factor — the method — is the one most open to improvement. It is the crucial factor, involving as it does both the teacher and the pupil. Questions of method will therefore take up the greater part of this book. If language teaching has greatly improved in the last thirty years, this has been mainly owing to the impact of new methodology on actual teaching in the classroom.

LANGUAGE TEACHING AS IT USED TO BE

When we look back on language teaching in the past, what is so striking is the absence, until about the beginning of the present century, of any kind of rigorous method, with the exception of course of great pioneers like Comenius[2] and François Gouin[3]. Method used to consist, above all, of grammatical rules and translation. The material in the text-book, and the order in which it was presented, were determined entirely by the author's predilections and personal experience. His decisions were taken from an adult point of view. Since the beginning of the century, education has benefited more and more from the rapid advancement of science. The study of psychology led to the creation of a new science, educational psychology, on which much of the theory and practice of modern teaching depend. The child is no longer treated as a minor adult. He is now seen as having a personality and interests of his own, as someone who needs to be active and free to take the initiative. School is no longer cut off from real life: it is wide open to the outside world. There has been a revolution in education, and language teaching has been affected by it like everything else in that area.

The principal innovation that occurred at the beginning of the century in the teaching of languages, throughout Europe, was the introduction of what became known as the Direct Method, an immediate result of the new psychology. What was the Direct Method all about? It meant teaching 'directly' in the foreign language, without the intermediary of the mother tongue, and demanding the active participation of the pupil, obliging him to use the new language himself from the start.

Unfortunately, the Direct Method suffered from the same defect as previous procedures, in that it exerted no control over the content and grading of the course. This is a fundamental point that we shall come to when we discuss the Direct Method as opposed to Audio-Visual Methods, which we shall take as an example of methods adopted more recently.

LANGUAGE TEACHING IN THE GENERAL ADVANCE OF SCIENCE

The essential thing about language teaching today is that a form of pedagogy that used to be considered an art is now becoming a science, so that we can justifiably begin to speak of the science of language teaching. We are thus carried along with the general advance of science in our times. There are some who feel that the advance has gone too far. Yet we should be wrong not to turn it to our advantage. Our profession has already been able to profit from several sciences that have made remarkable progress in recent decades, including anthropology, sociology and especially psychology, of which a relatively young branch, psycho-linguistics, could yield abundantly as far as we are concerned. The development of electronics has led to the production of better and better equipment that can take and store records of speech and then reproduce it exactly. However, there is one rapidly expanding science whose influence on language teaching has been of paramount importance, and that is linguistics.

LINGUISTICS

In tracing the history of linguistics, it is customary and right to recognise Ferdinand de Saussure[4] as the founder of the modern science, in so far as it dates from the publication of his famous *Cours de Linguistique Générale* in 1916. That does not mean that we should ignore all that had been done in this field from ancient times until then. On the contrary, Noam Chomsky[5], the outstanding figure in transformational linguistics, acknowledges his debt to the French linguists of the seventeenth century and the *Grammaire de Port-Royal*[6]. But it is true to say that Saussure began an important new era by opening the way for the development of structural linguistics[7], which has proved an extremely fruitful field. The value of Saussure's work has been well assessed by Malmberg[8]:

> "Most of the new movements in linguistics, which attach prime importance to descriptive studies, can be traced back more or less directly to Saussure. Thanks to his insistence on the synchronic method[9], linguistic description has won for itself a place of honour and is now generally accepted".

Let us consider some of the distinctive characteristics of twentieth century linguistics and see what use we can make of them in language teaching.

Modern linguistics is first of all *descriptive*[10], as Malmberg rightly reminds us; and from that standpoint it can be called an exact science. It is not concerned with constructing theories in the abstract. The linguist observes the phenomena of language and describes what he hears and sees, in much the same way as a scientist in a laboratory makes observations of and about the material before him.

Secondly — and this was an essential feature of Saussurian linguistics, although the idea itself was not new — modern linguistics concentrates on a *synchronic* study of language. Every language is constantly evolving: a synchronic study observes and describes one phase, supposedly stable, in the steady evolution. It is naturally the *contemporary language*, of which the linguist hears and sees evidence around him, that he is best placed to describe.

A third point, on which there is general agreement in twentieth-century linguistics, is the importance of describing the *spoken language* and all that speech entails. The oral language has many features that the written cannot adequately transcribe, and language, after all, is primarily speech.

Fourthly, a linguistic description makes it possible to reveal the particular *structure* of a language, which is different from the structure of every other language. Attempts have been made to identify 'universals' which appear to be common to a large number of languages; but the fact remains that each language operates in accordance with its own system of signals. We shall see, when we come to the chapter on Structural Drills, how productive the theory of structure can be when applied to language teaching.

THE INFLUENCE OF LINGUISTICS ON LANGUAGE TEACHING

Significant though these basic principles of modern linguistics are, years passed before they had any noticeable effect on language teaching, which remained tied, in Europe, to the Direct Method, and, in the United States, to the old grammar-translation method, at least until the last world war. Yet it was in the United States, where structural linguistics had forged ahead through the work of Sapir[11], Bloomfield[12] and many others, that language teaching, hitherto a long way behind Europe, really began to exploit linguistic research. In America, the demands of the second world war made it a matter of vital necessity that the teaching of languages should produce quick and positive results. Bloomfield himself was called upon to leave his linguistic researches for a time in order to take part in the teaching of foreign languages[13], and thus, incidentally, to become one of the founders of 'linguistics applied to language teaching'.

APPLIED LINGUISTICS

We shall be discussing 'linguistics applied to language teaching' and not simply 'applied linguistics', since linguistics can be applied for a variety of purposes, including telecommunications,

6

information theory, machine translation and speech therapy. Taking, then, only the application of linguistic notions to language teaching, let us see what its main principles are.

The most important, without any doubt, is the idea that we should begin by teaching the spoken language. In other words, our approach will essentially be oral. It is the oral form that linguists have mainly concentrated on in their descriptions; and they have thereby drawn attention to the difference in system and function between the spoken language and the written. This distinction has also been made by psychologists and neurologists, who have pointed out that certain pathological disturbances may affect one of the systems, leaving the other intact. We may therefore assume that language teaching is simplified if the two systems are treated separately, and that by starting with the spoken language we are following the natural, genetic and historical order. Language was, let us remember, spoken before it was written down.

A second important principle follows from the function of language as a means of communication between members of a community: it "meets the need for communication", as André Martinet[14] puts it. A foreign language course cannot be effective if it fails to satisfy that need. This adds support to the case for using dialogue as a starting point for beginners, as we shall see in Chapter Three.

Thirdly, linguists and psychologists are generally agreed in their belief that language can engage the user's entire behaviour. Physically, the ear and the mouth are chiefly concerned, so it is reasonable that modern methods should be audio-lingual. The hand comes into play, obviously, when writing begins — and not only then. The muscles of the face, and of other parts of the body too, help in the process of oral expression, in which gesture and mime play a prominent part. The use of language can, in fact, be an expression of the speaker's whole personality, and that is something the teacher can turn to good account.

A fourth principle derives from the independent and arbitrary nature of each language system. One consequence of this is that grammatical categories suitable for Greek and Latin are not necessarily appropriate for French and English. The learning of a foreign language will therefore be easier if the pupil is exposed directly and from the start to the system proper to that language, instead of being introduced to it through the medium of the mother tongue. This applies even — and indeed especially

— if the two languages are similar, since the likeness may be deceptive and may increase the chances of confusion. It is only at a later stage that a comparison between the foreign language and the mother tongue can be of practical value, though the teacher and the text-book writer must have it clear in their minds when planning their work.

In the structure of a language, the full significance of each linguistic item depends on the contrast that can be made between that item and others. Teaching will accordingly be a matter of making such contrasts evident at every level — phonological, grammatical and lexical — and of giving the pupil ample opportunities for practising them.

Similar principles can be applied to mother tongue teaching; and there is a growing awareness of this, in France and in other countries, notably in Britain and the United States where entirely new methods of teaching English have been worked out in the light of linguistic research. An important difference arises with the teaching of a foreign language in so far as consideration must be given to the pupil's first language and its constant tendency to interfere with the second. At the same time, we must take into consideration any true similarities there may be between the two languages — anything they really have in common that will help the learner along.

THE LIMITATIONS OF LINGUISTICS AS APPLIED TO LANGUAGE TEACHING

While we should realise the importance of linguistics for language teaching, we should equally recognise the difficulties of putting linguistic theories into practice in the classroom. The contribution that linguistics can make to language teaching is limited, and we should see clearly where the limits lie. They are imposed by the complexity and specific requirements of language teaching, which are themselves matters for investigation by the linguist, the psycho-linguist and the educational psychologist.

For the text-book writer, the problem of applying linguistics is two-fold:

> One: he has to select, from a vast accumulation of linguistic studies and a tangle of conflicting theories, whatever may be of practical use to him;

Two: he has to bear in mind the dichotomy in every act of teaching, which must consist of teaching *something*, and, at the same time, of teaching *somebody*; and he must always remember that the pupil may be more or less motivated, more or less receptive, more or less capable of language learning.

WHERE, THEN, IS THE RELEVANCE OF LINGUISTICS TO OUR WORK?

Its relevance has not always been apparent. This accounts for the long delay before language teachers began to take a serious interest in the subject, before they could be convinced that their profession might be more of a science than an art. Even today, the aims of the linguist are far removed from those of the language teacher, who, trying to understand a scholarly linguistic publication, has often had cause to wonder how it can possibly be related to the actual classroom situation. As a matter of fact, the linguist is usually not interested in the pedagogical problems involved in teaching the languages he analyses and describes. Noam Chomsky's declaration[15], at a language teaching conference in America, that linguistics had nothing to offer to the teaching of languages, came as a shock to many members of our profession.

Fortunately, Chomsky's argument was exaggerated. Whether linguistics and language teaching are seen to be related or not, the fact remains that the first has already made a very positive contribution to the second. Since the end of the nineteenth century, language teaching has certainly gained from Viëtor's[16] work on phonetics, as it did, when the present century began, from the studies of Rousselot[17] and Passy[18] in France, and later of Daniel Jones[19] in England. In Britain, H. E. Palmer[20] blazed a trail for new methods of language teaching; and the linguistic school of J. R. Firth[21] had a profound effect on language teaching attitudes. In America, especially during the second world war, the influence of Sapir, Bloomfield, Fries[22] and Delattre[23] was even greater. The relationship between linguistics and language teaching has been the outcome of an irreversible trend. Chomsky himself could not stop certain of his followers[24] applying his transformational theories in materials designed for language learning. In fact, it is now widely agreed that a thorough course in linguistics should form part of the training of every language teacher, and we shall elaborate on this in Chapter Seven. Moreover, it is difficult to imagine how any text-book writer could now compile language teaching materials without taking linguistic analysis fully into account.

But there we are faced with another problem. What linguistic theory is the text-book writer to rely on, when there are almost as many different theories as there are linguists, when each theory has its own terminology and is at some points in complete opposition to another theory on the same subject? That dilemma is brought out very well by W. F. Mackey[25] in Part One of his *Language Teaching Analysis*. In that monumental work, Professor Mackey begins by giving us a picture of the incredible proliferation of linguistic theories and the innumerable contradictions in them. For example, the principal phoneticians who have described spoken English, far from agreeing on one set of phonetic symbols, have used no fewer than thirteen different systems of transcription. A similar measure of disagreement is to be found over what used to be called the 'parts of speech'. Taking only six of the twentieth century linguists, Mackey presents us with a very revealing table which shows that their ideas vary from almost traditional views such as those of A. A. Hill[26], who retained seven word-categories in place of the old nine, to those of C. C. Fries, who rejected the nine traditional categories altogether. Fries disallowed even such terms as 'article', 'noun', 'pronoun' and 'adjective', and admitted only two word-categories — (i) *form-classes*, numbered 1 to 4, and (ii) *function words*, of which there were fifteen groups, labelled A to O.

Fundamental divergencies, both in theory and terminology, are found even in the main levels of linguistic analysis, e.g. phonology, morphology, syntax, lexicology. While Z. S. Harris[27] classifies all linguistic items under only two main headings, phonology and morphology, Brøndal[28] needed as many as fourteen! It is clear, too, that words as common as 'grammar', 'morphology' and 'syntax' refer to quite different areas of reality according to the writers who use them.

Anyone, therefore, who attempts to apply the abstractions of linguistics to the actual job of teaching a language in class, has good reason to feel baffled and to wish there were more harmony, more uniformity, in the jungle of modern linguistics. The author setting out to write a text-book for learners of French or English does not want dozens of different linguistic theories. What he needs, first of all (though he may not get it for a long time), is a good description of French or English — clear, precise, strictly accurate, complete; and then a practical comparison between the language to be taught and the pupil's mother tongue. Failing to piece together either of these things from the linguistic jigsaw, should he give up in despair and go back to the bad old ways, and the days when the scientific approach was regarded with uncomprehending mistrust, and when the teacher preferred his own 'intuitive' knowledge of the language? Certainly not; but we cannot hide the fact that the alternative to that retrograde step demands much more reading and preparation than before, both from the text-book writer and from the teacher using an up-to-date course-book conscientiously.

As for the teacher, he should constantly bear in mind three essentials that can help him out of the dilemma:

(a) His job is not to teach linguistics. It is to *teach a language*, to help other people to use that language correctly. It is not to give information *about* the language. The very multiplicity of linguistic theories should be sufficient to convince him of the wisdom of teaching through *practice* rather than through theory; for which of all the theories is he to teach?

(b) He is not bound by any one theory, in contrast with his linguistic colleague who is usually obliged to belong to one particular school. He can — and should — be perfectly free to choose, and to build up his work with the aid of any notion that may serve his ends. We shall see how that can be done when we come to discuss structural drills. There is a whole range of drills that he can make use of according to specific needs and circumstances; and variety is a vital element in good teaching. Some of the drills we shall be talking about — the many kinds of substitution exercises, for example — are based on the tagmemic models of Pike[29] and Longacre[30]. Others, such as exercises in expansion and reduction, are applications of the theory of immediate constituents[31]. The concept of transformational grammar[32] has been borrowed for the transformation exercises, e.g. on the negative and the passive.

Thus, rather than fish in only one linguistic stream, we should cast our pedagogical net in all waters that might bring us in a profitable catch.

(c) Above all, the language teacher is not concerned with linguistic matters only. He has to work with human beings, and his problems are as much psychological as linguistic. He should therefore expect from linguistics no more than that particular science can offer, always remembering that he can only draw from it, at the most, certain observations about the raw material of *what* he has to teach — and of what *parts* of it he needs to teach, for he can never cover it all. But linguistics can give him very little help when he has to decide *how to present* the material he has chosen to deal with. That is where he needs the psychology of learning — if it is indeed true that the teacher can do no more than assist the natural learning processes.

THE IMPORTANCE OF PSYCHOLOGY

What was said in the previous paragraph brings us to the question of language learning psychology, and to a brief consideration of some of the developments in that field which seem most noteworthy.

Some of us may have heard, a few years ago, of the dismay among language teaching experts in the United States — there were repercussions of it in Europe — when they realised that new methods, even the soundest from a linguistic point of view, were just not giving the expected results. It was then that they made a 'discovery'; they 'found out' that teaching involves not only the subject matter but also the person who is trying to learn. So voices were raised in support of the learner, and a greater attention to psychology was called for. Psycho-linguists were consequently invited to help solve the problems of learning and teaching languages, both native and foreign. Fervent researches were carried out, and are still in progress, in that domain. Much remains to be done; but already we have been given some idea of the mental processes through which the young child learns his own language, and this information is casting light on the acquisition of a second tongue.

The psychological matters that directly concern the language teacher include those of perception, memory, the establishment and reinforcement of behaviour patterns, the ability to think in abstract and general terms, the whole problem of motivation, and so on. Psychology has much to say on the question of the age at which one is best able to learn a new language. Ever since Piaget[33], we have had a clear picture of how the child's mind develops year by year. We can tell, for each age, the relative average capacity for perception, for imitation, association between the idea and the expression of it, and abstract reasoning. Thanks to Piaget and those who succeeded him, we know much more than our forebears did of the child's interests at each stage of his development and of the best time to start learning a foreign language.

Above all, we now fully realise that, whatever the age, no one really learns without wanting to; and this brings us back to the question of motivation. It is precisely this problem that produces a clash between linguistic and psychological demands; and here a compromise must be made. Purely linguistic considerations would prompt us to split language up into its basic elements, which would then be taught progressively, beginning with the phoneme, going on to the morpheme, the word, the clause, the sentence and so on to the paragraph. Such a procedure would also satisfy the pedagogical principle which, roughly speaking, favours progression from the simple to the complex. However, experience shows that association between the signifier and the signified, and the memorising of structures, are made much easier by a more synthetic approach which allows the items to be presented in real situations, which are more satisfying to the learner and enable him to apprehend the meaning and the form of the expression simultaneously.

With pupils and students of a foreign language, motivation can be created and fostered in a variety of ways, for example:

    (a) through the intrinsic interest of the texts selected;

    (b) through the appeal of the type of activity expected of the learner — games with young children, mime and dramatisation with older ones, rationalisation of the material taught at a later stage;

    (c) through an obvious correlation between such activity and the 'terminal behaviour' — the end product we hope to obtain;

(d) by arousing interest in cultural works associated with the language studied, whether those works resemble or contrast with those associated with the mother tongue;

(e) lastly — and this is too often forgotten — through the sense of achievement that comes from being able to use a foreign language effectively. To adopt Chomsky's terminology, it is *performance* that interests the learner, rather than *competence*, unless perhaps the learner happens to be studying linguistics.

Those are only a few of the lessons to be learnt from what might be called 'applied psychology in language teaching'. Like the lessons to be learnt from applied linguistics, they apply as much to the planning of a language text-book as they do to the classroom techniques employed by the teacher.

LANGUAGE DIDACTICS

Thus, long regarded as an art, language teaching has changed radically in the course of this century and has already acquired, at its best, a sense of scientific control. It has for some years now sheltered under the protective wing of the science of linguistics. But when it starts calling itself 'applied linguistics', linguists themselves are apt to look upon it with suspicion. 'Pure' linguists are inclined to be critical of the way in which language teaching adapts their theories to suit its practical ends. On the other hand, language teachers have felt uneasy in the guise of linguists, albeit applied. They know that their work has as much to do with psychology; yet, if they called themselves 'applied psychologists', that might bring them into disfavour with the psychologists too. Should not language teaching, therefore, set itself up as a discipline in its own right, without denying the invaluable support it has received from modern linguistics and from the other sciences to which it is indebted?

If so, what should the new discipline be called? The title of Robert Lado's book *Language Teaching: A Scientific Approach*[34] contains the elements of a suitable name, though of course it will not do as it is. Why not adopt Mackey's term *'language didactics'*? In any case, it will be various aspects of a discipline with such a label that we shall be examining in the following pages.

Part 1
METHODOLOGY

Chapter 2

Methods: Direct and Audio-Visual

The next four chapters deal with the methodology of foreign language teaching. In Chapter Two, the author begins with an enquiry into the meaning of method, and he is careful to explain that 'method' implies far more than 'technique'. He describes, with favour, Audio-Visual methods in general and compares them with the 'Direct Method' which was very much in the fashion earlier in this century and is still, though with considerable modification, widely used. It will be clear that the 'Audio-Visual Methods', as Denis Girard describes them, include some of the most important ideas that are now increasingly applied in current language teaching, ideas that go far beyond the mere technique of showing pictures accompanied by commentary on a tape-recorder. Girard attaches great importance to the philosophy underlying the methods he advocates, and claims strong support for them from linguistics and psychology.

We would all agree that *method* is a vital factor in the complex process of teaching a foreign language. Unfortunately, the term *method* is ambiguous. In English, the word usually refers to *a manner of teaching*. But it can also be used in one of the senses of the French word *méthode*, to indicate a text-book or a set of *teaching materials*. W. F. Mackey, who is completely bilingual in English and French, has come under fire from British and American colleagues for committing a gallicism by using *method* in that special sense of *méthode*. In fact, it is in that restricted sense that Mackey uses the term when he writes, in the book we referred to earlier and in other publications of his, about *method analysis*.

We shall see in this present chapter that methods need to be clearly distinguished from *techniques*.

Certain writers on the subject have tried to bring order into this confusion of terminology. Halliday, McIntosh and

Strevens[1] suggest abandoning the term *methodology*, which they feel has become corrupted, and adopting instead the word *methodics*, the suffix *-ics* supplying a nicely scientific note. They would then allow *method* to be used in a less technical, more general sense. In an article in *English Language Teaching*[2], E. M. Anthony proposes that a clear distinction should be made between three terms:

> (a) *approach*, as in 'oral approach', which would indicate 'a point of view, a philosophy, an article of faith';
>
> (b) *method,* which would cover a general plan for the presentation of the linguistic items to be taught; and
>
> (c) *techniques*, which would indicate tricks of the trade that the teacher practises in the classroom.

As Anthony sees it, the *technique* must accord with the *method*, which in its turn will be the outcome of a certain *approach*.

The reader will perhaps forgive this brief investigation into the meaning of terms we so often use. It may at least serve to introduce a discussion of two of the most commonly practised 'methods' in language teaching today — the 'Direct' and the 'Audio-Visual'.

WHAT DOES 'AUDIO-VISUAL' MEAN?

'Audio-visual' is one of those new-fangled terms that are bandied about and are given so much publicity that we all adopt them, feeling that they carry the prestige of a new technique — for this is an age when techniques play an increasingly dominant part in our lives.

'Audio-visual' was first used as an adjective. We spoke of 'audio-visual aids'. The "Audio-Visual Centre" of the Ecole Normale Supérieure at Saint-Cloud, near Paris, came into being just after the second world war. In that context, the adjective 'audio-visual' already covered a wide range of activities, involving every aspect of education.

Now, in France at any rate, we speak of 'the audio-visual', making the term into a noun. This only adds to the confusion it causes in our minds, and to the aura of magic and the miraculous in which certain modern teaching and communication techniques have become shrouded. The noun now embraces all mass media, every type of equipment used to reproduce sound and pictures, and at the same time all kinds of teaching materials designed for every level from the kindergarten to the university and professional training.

Restricting ourselves to modern language teaching, we find at least three main applications of the term:

1. In some cases, it is used as a label for a method of modern language teaching that uses auditory and visual aids, especially for mass instruction, and above all by television.

2. In other cases it is applied in a rather muddled way to the exploitation of the language laboratory, and is used to imply a kind of "press-button teaching", to indicate either approval or the opposite.

3. Thirdly, it suggests a whole range of techniques used more or less intensively within the framework of the normal language lesson in class.

In this chapter, we shall concentrate on the third sense of the term audio-visual as applied to language teaching, distinguishing in that sense between two practical applications:

1. the occasional use of audio-visual aids, either
   (a) purely visual aids, including illustrations of all kinds, projected or otherwise, and pictures that can be stuck on a flannel board; or
   (b) purely auditory aids, such as radio, record-players and tape-recorders, used by themselves or linked together in different types of language laboratory; or
   (c) a combination of the two, as in the cinema or on television.

2. the regular use of the 'integrated audio-visual method', as we have now come to call it. This implies the synchronised use of the tape-recorder and a visual aid, the latter generally being a film-strip or a flannel board.

It is impossible to draw a clear line of distinction between what we have found it convenient to call the 'Direct Method' and what we might now call the 'Audio-Visual'.

In point of fact the 'Direct Method' – as defined at the beginning of this century when it gradually became adopted in a great many countries, particularly in France and elsewhere in western Europe – seems to be more of the nature of a pedagogical approach than of a proper method of language teaching. It can be described quite simply as a way of teaching *directly* in the foreign language, without using the pupils' mother tongue. We all know that the main principle was not applied literally for very long and that the mother tongue was, in practice, often introduced through translation into or from the pupils' own language. The mother tongue was also resorted to in the teaching of grammar. But the chief weakness in the Direct Method was, as suggested in the previous chapter, that it laid down no rules on a question now regarded as fundamental, namely: *What* should be taught? As practised, the Direct Method left the teacher completely free to use as much of the foreign language as he liked, in any order.

We spoke, then, of the Direct Method; but we cannot speak of the 'Audio-Visual Method' in the same way. If by 'Audio-Visual Method' we mean no more than using a tape-recorder and a projector, that is misusing the word 'method': all we are doing in that case is employing a particular *technique*. There is not *an* audio-visual method: there are audio-visual *methods*, which consist of various combinations of teaching procedures that use, among other things, audio-visual equipment and are founded on certain methodological principles. There may be a considerable difference between one audio-visual method and another. However, in spite of the differences, it is possible to pick out certain ideas that the various methods have in common and to produce a tentative definition of *audio-visual methodology* which will cover a much wider area than that covered by a simple technique.

The aim of the present chapter is to try to formulate such a definition. In the process, we must examine the underlying *linguistic* and *psychological* theories. If indeed the mere technical media that we put into operation have an important part to play, their efficacy is largely the result of applying a combination of theoretical assumptions and scientific concepts that are our only real justification for using the word 'method' in this context.

THE LINGUISTIC BASIS

Every modern method of language teaching, audio-visual or not, and including what the Americans have called 'the New Key', is based on the much clearer insight into the language taught that we owe to twentieth century linguistics. That requires detailed explanation for which now is not the time. However, it is worth considering five of the essential contributions of linguistics that are relevant to our present theme:

1. Linguistics has provided *scientific descriptions* of *contemporary languages.* In other words, it has produced synchronic analyses of them. Such analyses entail:

   (a) isolation of the *basic elements* of a language, at different levels of analysis, the elements having *distinctive features* that can be identified and contrasted with one another;

   (b) *measurement* of the results of analysis whenever possible – for example by studying the frequency of occurrence and the distribution of the phonic elements (e.g. phonemes and syllable-types), of the lexical items and even of grammatical structures;

   (c) study of the *combination or ordering of these elements* within a language as it is used: in other words, study of the basic *structure* of the language.

2. It has provided a means of scientific comparison between one language and another, identifying the distinctive features of each language system, the essential differences between them, and also the similarities (this touches on the delicate and highly debatable question of language 'universals').

3. It has drawn attention to the primary importance, in any language, of *speech*, the *language spoken.* In the origin and historical development of a language, speech naturally came first. It has many characteristics that are represented in the written language inadequately or not at all; and the spoken and written styles often follow different conventions.

4. It attaches importance to *communication* as an essential function of language. Without being too dogmatic, we can perhaps agree in the main with Martinet[3] when he said that every language "satisfies the need for communication in a community". With this in mind, the linguist carries his researches into the field of sociology, so that now the science of socio-linguistics is opening up a vast territory hitherto practically unexplored.

5. It also attaches importance to the idea that the use of language is *a form of behaviour* which may involve the whole personality of the user, and that, in such behaviour, psychometric habits may be just as much involved as the intellectual faculties. In this, the psychologists confirm the discoveries of the linguist, particularly in their studies of the processes of language acquisition. We shall return to the psychological aspect of language function later.

In so far as these five points concern modern language teaching in general, each of them can be applied directly to teaching by audio-visual means. Thus:

1. The *basic linguistic items*, of which the text-book writer will have made an inventory with the help of such linguistic analyses as are available to him, will not be taught in isolation, but always with regard to their *structural combination or ordering*. An audio-visual method will only teach complex structures which are at once phonological, morphological and syntactic.

2. A *comparison* between the pupils' mother tongue and the 'target language' will be used to justify, at least in part, the choice of the linguistic items taught and the order in which they are presented in the course.

3. An adequate command of the *spoken language* will be the first aim of every audio-visual method: comprehension of written texts, and the writing of original composition, will not be expected of the pupil until the foundations of oral proficiency have been firmly laid.

4. Every audio-visual method will operate through *dialogue*, since this provides an example of language functioning as *communication*.

5. Finally, in audio-visual methodology the formation of *linguistic habits* will always precede theoretical discussion of the language learnt.

THE PSYCHOLOGICAL BASIS

We have already noted how psychology can, at certain points, lend its support to the linguist. We must consider that point in more detail, as the psychological basis of audio-visual teaching is of the greatest importance.

Psychology can be called upon to support linguistics in a description of two sectors of our field:

1. linguistic communication;
2. the learning process,
   (a) of the mother tongue,
   (b) of a foreign language.

Communication (that essential function of language) can be considered as a two-way operation of *encoding* and *decoding*, on the following simple pattern:

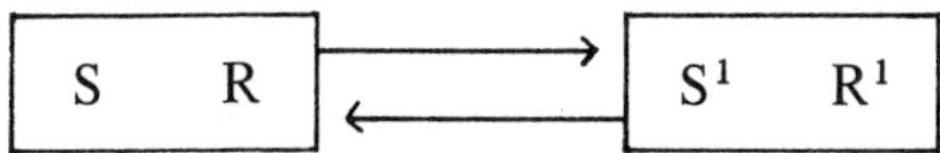

where S R and S^1 R^1 stand for two 'senders-receivers', who will be speakers-hearers in the case of an oral code, writers-readers in the case of a written one.

For this two-way operation to take place, two essential conditions must be fulfilled:

1. the two participants must have concepts in common, for which they need expression;
2. they must have at their disposal an agreed *code*, that is to say a system of *signals* which they can use or refer to at any time in order to make up or decipher a message. This code will be understood despite idiosyncracies of accent and manner of speaking, or what experts in communication call mere 'noise'.

In most languages, there is in fact a dual code, one part oral, one part written.

In mother tongue acquisition, it is assumed that the child learns to *listen* and to *speak*, then to *read* and *write*. In other words, he learns to receive (or perceive) messages, and to interpret them. These messages will be first oral, then written, i.e. the child learns first to listen before speaking, and to read before writing. Later he learns to *encode* and transmit similar messages himself. In every civilisation and with every individual person, this process of learning to transmit takes place in two phases: we first learn to speak, later to write.

The faculties brought to bear on the four-phase process of listening, speaking, reading, writing — the four basic skills of language learning — are of two kinds:

1. psycho-physiological (perceptive and motor); and

2. intellectual (analytical and creative).

They seem to operate at three levels, which can be illustrated in the following diagram which I have borrowed from Professor Pit Corder's book *The Visual Element in Language Teaching*[4], and slightly adapted:

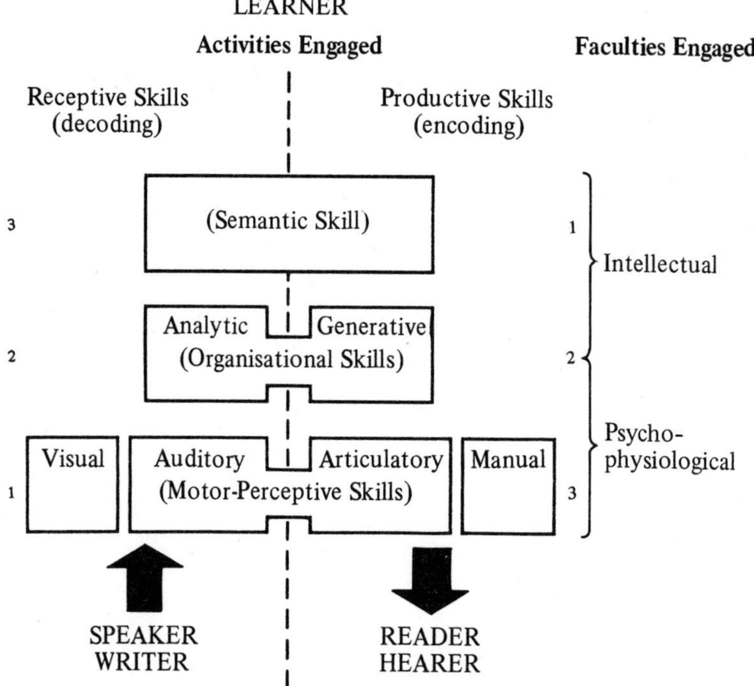

In acquiring a new language, the learner, we assume, undergoes a similar experience. However, the formation of new linguistic habits is obstructed by the already firmly established habits of the mother tongue. The *interference* so caused raises two kinds of problems that have to be solved:

1. They may be of a *socio-cultural* nature. To take one simple example, names for the days of the week, such as Friday, Saturday, Sunday in English, or *vendredi, samedi, dimanche* in French, may cause confusion according to whether they are being used in a Moslem, Jewish or Christian community[5].

2. They may be strictly *linguistic*. In that case, interference may occur

    (a) in the oral system of the language, so that, for example, an English-speaker learning French will pronounce French vowels as if they were English diphthongs, and will put stress where and when it is not required in a French word or sentence; or

    (b) in the written system, especially when the L1 (the child's first language) and L2 (the second language) use the same alphabet but apply it to different phonological systems.

The 'traditional' way of teaching modern languages (and I am referring particularly to the so-called Direct Method as, more often than not, it is still practised) fails to take the findings of psychological research sufficiently into account. Hence:

    (a) it tends in general to present too many difficulties at a time, and, in particular, to teach the spoken language and the written simultaneously, or at least with too short a period of transition;

    (b) it makes inadequate use of dialogue, giving preference to the language of description, which does not happen to serve the same purposes of communication. Descriptive style plays a minor role in the vocal exchanges of everyday life, a role far less important than it is given in the Direct Method;

(c) it makes too many demands on purely mental activity, and too few on the psycho-physiological faculties, even when it claims to be concentrating on 'active' learning.

(d) it fails to avoid L1 interference, partly because it does in fact resort frequently to translation, and partly because of the widespread practice of teaching the structures of the foreign language, throughout the course, *via* the structures of the mother tongue.

Up-to-date language teaching (audio-visual or otherwise) takes these psychological factors more fully into consideration. It aims first and foremost at providing, by every possible means, those conditions for learning which are valid for every language and which are particularly suitable for learning a foreign tongue. In any case, is not 'providing conditions for learning' the best definition — both modest and ambitious, and above all realistic — of what 'teaching' really is? In the present context, that definition implies, in the elementary stages:

(a) highlighting the oral system and letting the written come later;

(b) treating language frankly as a form of behaviour rather than as an abstract mental exercise;

(c) constantly creating the need for communication;

(d) avoiding, in classroom practice, all reference to the mother tongue.

Audio-visual methods of teaching apply the lessons of modern educational psychology. They pay as much attention as possible to the faculties of perception, auditory discrimination and clear oral production, allowing all of these to develop out of *dialogue about a real situation*. They have the advantage of having at their service a *technique* that enables them to achieve their ends more easily, more rapidly and more permanently.

26

This technique consists of using:

> (a) *supporting visual material* which is evocative and which ensures comprehension (or decoding of the message) without the aid of the mother tongue.

> (b) *a combination of this supporting visual material and a recording of the real spoken language*, which reproduces authentically the kind of conditions under which the L1 is learnt, while making due allowance for the need to avoid L1 habits.

The two diagrams on pages 28 and 29 illustrate how the L2 learning process operates, first with the traditional form of Direct Method, then with the Audio-Visual. In the diagrams, L1 stands for 'mother-tongue', L2 for 'the foreign or target language', C for 'concept', and E for the linguistic 'expression' of C.

The chief merit of an audio-visual method, as we can see immediately by comparing the two diagrams, is that it does not allow L1 to enter into the circuit at all. The encoding-decoding operation takes place in two stages instead of three, and com-prehension comes direct through C2, without the risk of socio-cultural interference — provided, of course, the supporting visual material projects the right image.

We can also see from the diagrams that audio-visual methods cut out interference, oral or written, in E2, as there is no link between E2 and E1; and they avoid confusion between C1 and C2, when the two concepts are not identical.

In teaching by an audio-visual method, it is possible to set up a kind of 'conditioned reflex'. The oral message contained in E2, on the tape, acts as a 'natural stimulus' that prompts the pupil to repeat what he hears and thus to encode straight into L2; and the supporting visual material encourages this process. After a certain time, the teacher stops the tape-recorder and projects the picture on to the screen without the accompanying sound. The picture then acts as an 'artificial stimulus' and triggers off a reflex action, so that the pupil automatically produces E2 — the expression in the foreign language — without the help of the 'natural stimulus', the tape-recording. In a way, this is rather like what happens when a child learns his mother tongue. He learns to say 'Mummy', 'Daddy' and other words, when certain persons or familiar objects appear before him. Then, when he is shown a picture of the persons or objects without their being physically present, he reacts by uttering their names just as if they were there. Such an experience is an exciting and impressive one when children are learning to speak. The comparable experience in L2 learning, encoding straight into E2 simply at the sight of a picture, can be just as exciting to the pupil and can leave a lasting impression.

FOREIGN LANGUAGE LEARNING PROCESS

1. **By one of the traditional methods: Diagram 1**

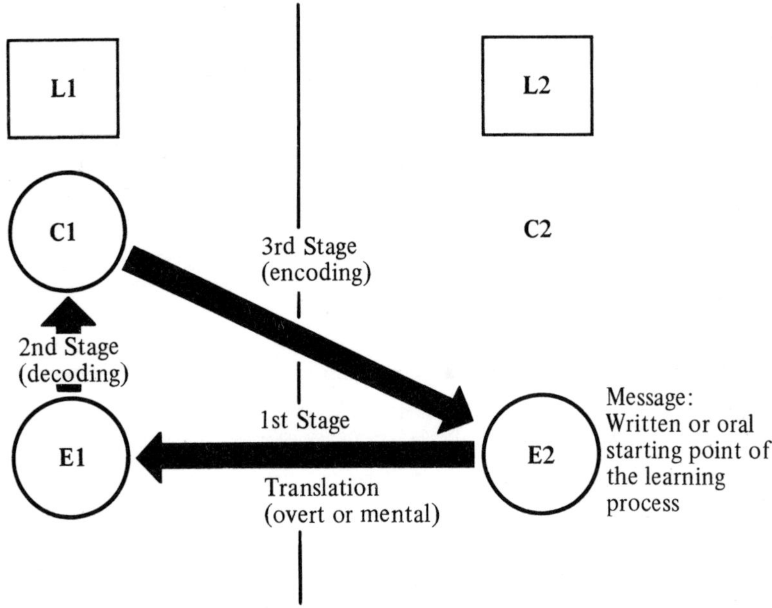

N.B. This assumes that C1 and C2 are identical. When they are not, the learning process, by missing out C2 altogether, cannot avoid creating socio-cultural confusion.

28

2. By an audio-visual method: Diagram 2

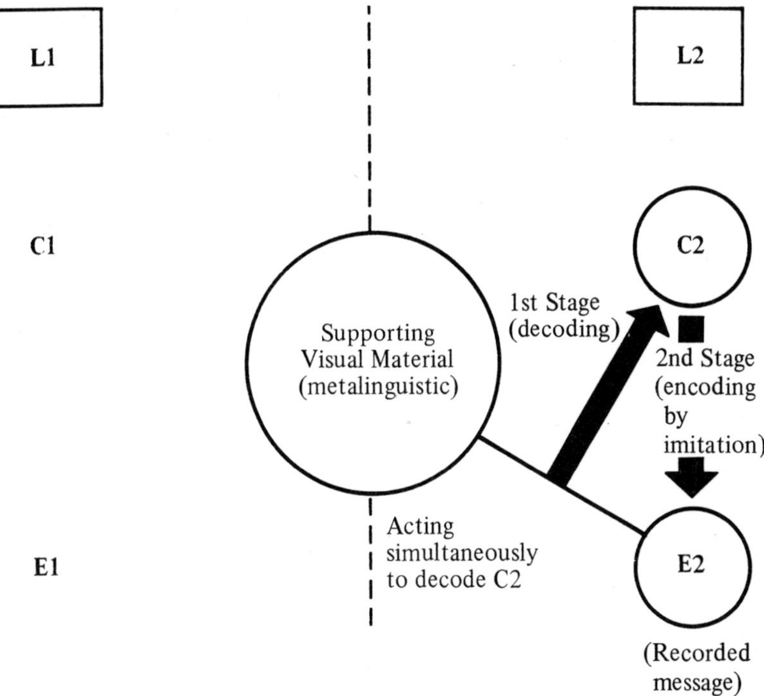

N.B. In this case C1 and E1 are right out of the circuit.

BASIC PRINCIPLES OF THE AUDIO-VISUAL METHODS

The rest is relatively easy. The basic principles of the audio-visual methods follow quite naturally from the linguistic and psychological ideas we have already discussed.

CONTENT OF THE COURSE
(methodological aspect of the lesson)

The content of the course will only be decided on the basis of a proper *analysis* of L2, and with due attention, as far as possible, to a comparison with L1.

The presentation of linguistic items will always be made in *complete utterances*, with concentration first on the phonological component, then on the grammatical, then on the lexical, in that order.

These utterances will be presented in *dialogue about a real situation*, a dialogue so composed as to let the pupils identify themselves with the 'characters in the play', as it were. This will provide them with the *need for communication*, supplying them at the same time with the means of meeting that need.

Plenty of exercises will then be given with the object of establishing command of the basic *structures* that form the skeleton of the dialogue with which the learning process began.

TEACHING TECHNIQUES (pedagogical aspect of the lesson)

We shall consider four quite different types of technique, each having a clearly defined aim:

1. *Intensive aural-oral work*, with a gradual withdrawal of the auditory aid (by stopping the tape-recorder), then of the visual aid. At this stage, careful attention should be paid to the phonetic quality of the pupils' own efforts in the L2, and to both the prosodic and the phonemic aspects of it. The objective at this stage is that the pupils should retain a good auditory image of the original dialogue, which they will have understood with the help of the supporting visual materials.

2. *Systematic structural exercises*, which have the virtue of pattern drill and the added advantage of being fully contextualised, since they will deal solely with the structures learnt in the natural living context of the dialogue.

3. *Application* of the linguistic items already learnt by heart. This will give the pupils an opportunity of making the items 'their own words' and of using them for whatever they want to say on their own. The object now is to get away from the inevitable parrot-like repetition of the first stage, to achieve an increasing independence of expression and to arrive at a spontaneous use of the L2, comparable with normal speech in the L1.

4. *Introduction of the written language* after a period which will vary in length according to the particular form of method employed, but which will rarely be shorter than fifty hours of aural-oral work, allowing ample time for a thorough assimilation of the basic structures.

THE PLACE OF AUDIO-VISUAL METHODS IN LANGUAGE
TEACHING

It cannot be denied — and indeed it is now less and less in
dispute— that audio-visual methods, as described in this chapter,
have a very important part to play in teaching foreign languages,
especially at the beginners' level. That level generally corres-
ponds with the first two years of secondary education, or more
or less the first 250 hours of foreign language learning.

However, conscientious teachers, impressed by the results
obtained during the elementary stages, often ask: "But what
next?" By this they usually have in mind: "Shall we not, at the
next stage, have to return to a more traditional type of teaching?"

The answer is in fact quite clear. I agree that the teacher and
the pupil must free themselves step by step from the restrictions
imposed by the audio-visual technique. Nevertheless, the linguistic, psychological and methodological principles that apply
at the beginning of the course remain valid at every stage of it.
It is only the *technique* that will change at the higher levels.
Thus:

(a) illustrations will become fewer but more complex.
    Instead of functional pictures, deliberately simpli-
    fied so as to serve no other purpose than to ensure
    comprehension of the relevant linguistic item in the
    most direct way, there will be more realistic, more
    photographic pictures, giving, for example, a de-
    tailed idea of this or that aspect of the civilisation
    associated with the language taught;

(b) recordings will likewise be used less frequently, but
    they will be more varied, and will present the
    students with different styles of the language.
    Graduating from passages written especially by the
    text-book writer to real texts written by recognised
    authors, the student will still begin with an aural
    experience of the text, listening to it before reading
    it himself and before doing written exercises on it;

(c) there will, of course, be a shorter and shorter inter-
    val between oral presentation of new material and
    the study of it on the printed page;

(d) training in original composition will become in-
    creasingly important and will be conceived as the
    normal extension of training in oral expression;

(e) more and more time will be devoted to the culture,
    including of course literature, associated with the
    language studied.

Seen in that light, there is surely no difference between the highest ultimate aims of traditional secondary education, which were to impart a knowledge of the culture of the people whose language was being studied, and what audio-visual methods are trying to accomplish. If the new objectives seem at first too practical, it is because, after all, only through a practical command of the language, which is an instrument of communication for practical use, can our objectives, however defined, be really attainable.

It is up to us, therefore, to decide what are the most reasonable steps, what are the techniques appropriate to each stage and in accordance with a positive methodological philosophy, by which we can achieve our ends with the maximum effect.

Chapter 3

Dialogue or Structure?

In the previous chapter, we were told: "The presentation of linguistic items will always be made in *complete utterances*. . . . These utterances will be presented in *dialogue about a real situation*". This raises a fundamental issue in language teaching: should we present the beginner with real, synthetic pieces of language, or should we start analytically, giving the pupil step by step the separate units that he can assemble at a later stage? Denis Girard examines the two sides of this question, and sees advantages and disadvantages in both. He concludes that a judicious combination of dialogue and structural grading is the best answer.

He illustrates his arguments with examples from the teaching of French as a foreign language, but for reasons explained in the General Introduction, I have translated most of these examples into English.

SHOULD THERE BE DIALOGUE?

The point at issue here is not the fruitful question-and-answer between teacher and pupil that is the essence of every good language lesson. What I want to do is to examine the arguments for and against using dialogue as a basis for the teaching of a foreign language — I mean as a model for the pupil to imitate and then to expand, with the object of acquiring an active command of the spoken tongue and eventually of the language in all its aspects. The point at issue, therefore, is whether we should use dialogue as a foundation for the linguistic content of the entire course and as a supporting structure for the lessons as they develop stage by stage.

The idea behind this inquiry came from a controversy that arose a short time ago across the Atlantic, in which those who advocated what might be called 'presentation through dialogue' took up the cudgels against the 'extreme structuralists' who maintained that a language should be taught basically as a series of linguistic structures[1]. Disagreement between the extremes of these two points of view is inevitable. There is bound to be a clash between a purely structural approach to language teaching, proceeding solely on linguistic grounds, and the approach of educational psychology. The former obliges the text-book writer and the teacher to keep to a strictly graded presentation of basic structures; the latter tries to reconcile linguistic realities with what is likely to interest the pupil. 'Presentation through dialogue' contains, itself, an inherent contradiction. Its disadvantages and dangers are undeniable; and it is worth while seeing if the advantages outweigh them.

A SUMMARY OF HOW THE 'DIALOGUE METHOD' WAS DEVELOPED

Enough has been written elsewhere about the old method, inherited straight from the teaching of Greek and Latin, of learning a language through lists of words, grammar and translation. The pupil was expected, by this method, not to make original use of the foreign language, but to interpret written texts and translate classic authors into his mother tongue. Dialogue had no part in such a method. A few text-book writers in the last century nevertheless felt the need to add to the translation exercises an appendix to which they gave the misleading sub-title 'Conversation'. This consisted of a series of questions on the text set for translation. A sentence like *A French officer who was travelling across Germany a long time ago, before railways had been invented, stopped at a wayside inn* would be the 'stimulus' for the following scrap of 'conversation':

> Question: What had not been invented?
> Answer: Railways.

And the author of that text-book was ahead of his times!

Yet, as a matter of historical fact, as early as the seventeenth century a school of linguists (in spite of being primarily Latinists) had foreseen the necessity of giving students practice in speaking living languages and of teaching them through actual. usage "rather than through a whole hotch-potch of rules and exceptions". Sieur du Tertre for instance, as early as 1651, was putting forward the idea, so popular with twentieth century linguists, that the chief function of a language is *communication.* He wrote: "Who would deny that men speak but to voice their thoughts or to elicit the thoughts of others?"[2].

That is quite a good definition of dialogue – but of the kind of dialogue that would be the ultimate aim of language teaching: it obviously could not be used for beginners.

About a hundred years ago, a French course appeared in Philadelphia composed entirely of dialogues graded according to difficulty[3]. The principle behind it was the one later put into practice so successfully by Assimil and Linguaphone. At the same time, François Gouin was launching *his* original method. It presented a language through situations associated with various human activities, beginning with gestures and very simple actions, which the teacher – who had to be both actor and commentator – described in a series of sentences, with the verb or the whole predicate prominent in each utterance. This was using, as the basis of the language lesson, not dialogue, but a monologue accompanying the performance of a sequence of actions. In this method, there was concern for a logical and graded presentation of language dealing with the realities of everyday life. In it can be seen the origins of the Active Method, and of the Direct Method as well, in so far as the lesson was given in the foreign language except for a few explanations in the mother tongue. The Minister of Education at the time, Victor Duruy, issued a circular that was a forerunner of the French Ministerial Instructions, in which he wrote: "The method to be followed is the one that I shall call the natural method, the one by which the family teaches a child his own tongue". So the model for foreign language teachers was to be the mother-and-child dialogue. Despite those recommendations and the example set by Sieur du Tertre and Gouin, the traditional *Grammar – Translation – Vocabulary* method continued to hold sway in the classroom. Can it be said to have been completely abandoned yet?

The Direct Method, which was so much in favour at the beginning of the century, established dialogue between teacher and pupils as the basis of all language teaching and forbade practically all resort to the mother tongue. It marked great progress along the road towards the 'natural method' so strongly advocated by Victor Duruy and put into practice by François Gouin. However, teachers who use the Direct Method tend to build up a dialogue artificially on written texts which they expect their pupils to paraphrase as best they can. There is no attempt at linguistic grading, nor are the pupils given any model of the spoken language that they can imitate.

It was not until linguistics began to exert an influence on language teaching that a decisive step in the right direction was taken. Behaviourist linguistics joined forces with the intuition and genius of François Gouin and Sieur du Tertre by insisting on the need to establish unconscious habits in the use of spoken language. Structural linguistics, through a scientific analysis and description of basic phonological and grammatical structures, provided the teacher and text-book writer with the foundation for a systematically graded presentation of their material. And that brings us back to the cause of the conflict referred to at the beginning of this chapter — the conflict between, on the one hand, a structural analysis which is essentially artificial (as any analysis is that aims at reducing real and complex phenomena to a limited number of elements), and, on the other hand, the attempt to recapture the full meaning of the speaker who uses the language in a natural synthetic act of communication.

At one of the extremes of this divergence, we had, for example, the school of the English Language Institute of Michigan under Charles Fries and Robert Lado, which came down firmly in favour of the structural method in 1941 and made pattern drill the keystone of all language teaching[4]. That was also the line taken, at the same period, by Pierre Delattre, who, with French, began by teaching all the phonemes in a sequence of sentences graded according to academic criteria but hardly offering models of natural conversation. One of his sentence   .n thus: *La belle demoiselle qui passe là-bas est la voisine de Jeanne à la classe de mathématiques de la capitale[5]*. (The beautiful young lady walking over there is the neighbour of Jean in the mathematics class in the capital.)

At the other extreme we had the exponents of the audio-visual methods (for example CREDIF[6], the Audio-Visual Centre at Saint-Cloud[7], and the University of Zagreb[8]) which presented a basic form of the spoken language through dialogues recorded on tape accompanied by film designed to illustrate the meaning of the dialogues and to help the student remember them. In spite of the name "structural-global" given to these methods by Professor Guberina[9], they were far removed from the pure structuralism preached by Fernand Marty. We can soon see the difference if we analyse the first dialogue in the course *Voix et Images de France*[10] which contains these grammatical structures: *Vous êtes* (You are) ... *Je suis* (I am) ... *Vous connaissez* (You know) ... *Entrez, s'il vous plait* (Come in, please) ... *Asseyez-vous* (Sit down) ... *M. T. est français* (Mr. T. is French) ... *Vous habitez à* (You live at) ... *J'habite* (I live) ... etc., with affirmative and interrogative intonations, and with already three-quarters of the French phonological system, namely twenty-seven phonemes, including the three nasal sounds /ã/, /õ/, /ɛ̃/, the contrasts /ɛ/v̠/e/, /ɛ/v̠/ɛ̃/, /ø/v̠/œ/, /a/v̠/ã/, /o/v̠/ɔ/, /o/v̠/õ/ and the consonant /R/.

The same comment can be made if we examine, for example, the first dialogue in *Pierre et Seydou*, a course produced by B.E.L.C.[11] for the teaching of French in English-speaking Africa. That dialogue contains the same number of phonemes and the same problem of the order in which new phonetic items are presented. However, the dialogue in this case is not introduced until there have been ten lessons initiating the learner into these phonetic difficulties; and the number of grammatical structures is noticeably smaller than in the first dialogue of *Voix et Images.*

The Dialogue Method, thanks especially to CREDIF, is now enjoying a great success in Europe and it has been developed considerably in North America during the last decade, despite the opposition of the pure structuralists and the believers in pattern drill. Professor Leopold Taillon has analysed thirty-six text-books for the teaching of French in current use in Canada and the United States and published between 1950 and 1963: two-thirds of them present the elements of the language in the first place through dialogue.

ARGUMENTS FOR AND AGAINST THE USE OF
DIALOGUE

Professor Taillon has listed the advantages and disadvantages of the dialogue method. The advantages are grouped under three headings:

1. **Psychological.** "The use of dialogues, especially if the situations they relate to are well illustrated, minimises the risk of interference by the mother tongue." "The dialogue method provides the best conditions for personal

participation by the pupil and therefore for the formation
of new habits."

2. **Pedagogical**. "We must admit that teaching a language
   through dialogue has proved itself. . . . The pupils,
   especially when they are beginners, are very keen to
   speak the new language."

3. **Linguistic**. "The principal aim is the spoken language,
   whose rules are not only different from those of the
   written, but much simpler."

Admittedly, it is debatable whether the spoken language
really is simpler than the written. What is certain is that the two
systems are different, and that often one difference is that the
written system contains a large number of redundant features:
this is especially so in the case of French[12]. Moreover, Professor
Taillon is careful to point out that in his opinion the advantages
are theoretical and potential, and depend on the way the dialogues are composed.

However, there is another considerable advantage of the
dialogue method that is not mentioned by Professor Taillon:
dialogue, when it is well constructed, and when it presents
linguistic structures in situation, makes it much easier for the
pupils to remember those structures.

If we now consider the drawbacks of the dialogue method,
we see that they can practically be reduced to a single one. This
has been very well stated by Professor Leo L. Kelly of Purdue
University, in an article in *The French Review* already referred
to, and quoted by Professor Taillon:

"By its very nature, dialogue rules out systematic presentation of language structure. Once a situational context for a
particular conversation has been decided on, the author is
obliged to make his characters say what is 'natural and normal'
in that situation." It is therefore impossible to build up the
language by putting one stone on top of another. You have to
put the construction together with pre-fabricated pieces.

According to Fernand Marty, the use of dialogue enables
the teacher to reach only the last two of the eight main objectives that he thinks should be aimed at in the French course for
beginners, and those two are the least important, namely:

1. to help the pupil understand and use, in certain situations, expressions which native speakers of the target

language normally use (e.g. *Have you anything to declare? Waiter, the bill, please*, etc.);

2. to give the pupil enough information about the foreign way of life to enable him to adapt himself to that life easily.

Monsieur Marty maintains on the other hand that the remaining six objectives are unattainable by the dialogue method. They are:

1. ability to handle syntactic and morphological structures so as to produce original and acceptable sentences;

2. mastery of an adequate vocabulary;

3. a pronunciation that makes all the phonological contrasts essential for effective communication;

4. normal fluency in speech;

5. ability to understand L2 speakers talking at normal speed;

6. correctness in spelling.

HOW DIALOGUE CAN BE USED EFFECTIVELY

I would like to emphasize that in my view dialogue should not be regarded as the essential structure of the course: it is only the foundation and the scaffolding. It is a means of presenting certain linguistic items, of making them comprehensible, of getting the pupils to imitate them in a meaningful context and to commit them to memory by dint of repetition. But such exercises form only one part of the language lesson. By beginning each unit of the course with a dialogue, I part company with Professor Taillon, who advocates using it as an exercise in the practical application of structures which have already been systematically taught; and what I propose differs from the later work of Fernand Marty, who first used the structural method and the dialogue method separately, and then decided that the best solution was to use the two methods concurrently and in parallel.

In support of my own position, I would simply say that in language teaching the psychological factors seem to me no less important than the linguistic ones. Language teachers who give priority to the learning of structures in isolation today, are making the same mistake as their predecessors: they are forgetting that most important element in all teaching — the attitude and reactions of the pupil. Just as traditional methods seem to proceed on the assumption that the pupil must become like his teacher, learning to think about the language and explain it, rather than learning simply to use it, so certain modern methods seem to be based on the belief that the pupil must become a linguist capable of describing the language being learnt. I would not aim as high as that, and definitely not in the elementary stages. It is of course dangerous to generalise, and the age and capacity of the pupil must always be borne in mind; but an essential factor that no teaching method can ignore is motivation. Unless one happens to be dealing with a special group of adults of a scientific turn of mind, then Fernand Marty's objective of forming "clear and logical general statements" about the foreign language is hardly likely to be the ambition of a class of beginners.

With most pupils, motivation can perhaps be fostered in three different but complementary ways. First, the content of the course should be relevant to the pupils' own concerns. Whatever text is used as a vehicle for the linguistic items to be taught, it should catch their interest; it should take them out of their own surroundings by showing them a picture of reality in a foreign, even exotic, environment; or it should do the opposite and give them a sense of reassurance by recalling some part of real life familiar to them. Secondly, one could exploit what might be called the productiveness of the linguistic items taught — the possibility of the pupils' being able to use them for their own ends and to use them again and again in similar situations. Thirdly, there is the powerful stimulus of the sense of achievement that comes with the ability to handle these items more or less correctly; and this, let us not forget, makes it well worth while getting the pupils to repeat and repeat and repeat, to a degree that might strike an outside observer as excessive.

Now it would be difficult to secure that three-fold motivation by using a method that excluded the presentation of more than one structure at a time. How can you hope to interest pupils in a foreign language by a lesson composed of a series of sentences of the type:

This is a book

This is an exercise-book

This is a boy

This is a dog

   etc. etc.?

If you reject dialogue as a basis for your lesson, you must either adopt the above sort of presentation, or you must choose a text in, say, descriptive style, i.e. composed of structures least likely to occur and to be useful in everyday conversation; while the most elementary form of dialogue will satisfy the innate need for communication common to all. For example:

Qui est-ce? C'est Jacques?	(Who is there? Is it Jack?)
Non, ce n'est pas Jacques.	(No, it isn't Jack)
C'est Simone?	(It's Simon?)
Oui, c'est Simone.	(Yes, it's Simon)
Entre, Simone.	(Come in, Simon)

The 'structuralists' will object that that little dialogue is swarming with difficulties. In French, it already contains some fifteen phonemes, including two nasal vowels which learners of many linguistic backgrounds will find hard to imitate. It presents the contrast between rising and falling intonation. As far as grammar is concerned, it contains four or five different structures. However, there is no question of analysing those structures: all the pupil is expected to do in the first place is to understand the meaning they convey and then to imitate them. Experience proves that, with most pupils, the ability to imitate can be relied upon when the need to imitate is active enough. Fernand Marty raises objections to the inclusion in elementary dialogue of such a harmless expression as *Comment allez-vous?* (How are you?), on the grounds that it has two dangerous pitfalls: the *t* of *comment*, normally silent, must be sounded before the *a* of *allez* in that greeting; and *allez*, usually meaning 'go', is there used in a special sense. But surely we need not take that objection seriously. All that is required at the beginning is (a) that the pupil should adequately reproduce the sound of the whole utterance [kɔmɑ̃talevu] and (b) that we can be sure he will use it meaningfully when he finds himself in a similar situation to the one reflected in the dialogue in which it occurred.

That touches on a very important aspect of the dialogue method properly used: the need to foresee a whole series of exercises which will follow the initial phase of understanding the dialogue and learning it practically by heart, and which will enable the pupil to assimilate the structures learnt and to establish them as new linguistic habits. If one stopped after the initial phase, it is true that all that would be achieved would be Fernand Marty's 'last two objectives', mentioned above. But the dialogue method, as I see it, rests on the principle that these exercises (which I have described in detail in Chapter Four, under the headings *Application* and *Reinforcement*) must follow the initial phase.

The 'Application' Exercises break away from rote learning and soon become something quite different from the simple substitution drills mentioned by Marty. They provide an opportunity for all kinds of 'transformations'[13] and a constructive 'generation' of sentences in the language, starting from the 'kernel sentences' in the original dialogue.

The 'Reinforcement' Exercises are no less essential as a means of ensuring a permanent assimilation of the different structures taught. Obviously, here we are going in the same direction as the 'structuralists', but without the boredom, since the structures we shall be exercising are parts of a genuine, living dialogue: they are useful and exploitable in communication, which is the true reward for all the effort of mastering a foreign language. One might argue that it is difficult to provide exercises covering all the structures introduced in the dialogue. But that, I suggest, is purely a matter of how you plan your work. True, if you followed the old practice of simply setting exercises on one or two points of grammar arising out of the text (in this case, the dialogue), and squeezed these in at the end of the lesson, the structures could not be assimilated properly. But if you spent twice as long on application and reinforcement exercises as on learning the dialogue − as you should, as a general rule − then the exercises should have lasting effect. Admittedly, it would be neither possible nor desirable to deal systematically with every single structure occurring in the dialogue and to provide for pronunciation exercises on, say, each one of the twenty-seven phonemes occurring in the first dialogue of *Voix et Images de France* or of *Pierre et Seydou*. However, it is the text-book writer's business to plan the exercises in such a way as to provide a skilful grading that will step by step cover all the main problems, and will eventually enable the learner to master all the phonological and grammatical structures and the basic lexical items of the language. In the case of *Pierre et Seydou*, for example, the Teacher's Book devotes ten pages to application and reinforcement exercises for practice in the principal structures of the first dialogue alone. It should also be pointed out that the number of new structures in the first few dialogues is comparatively high. The ratio of the number of structures introduced in each dialogue to the total number in the book decreases as the course proceeds and as mastery of new items becomes more important.

HOW TO COMPOSE THE DIALOGUES

We have been discussing what use can be made of dialogues in teaching. It is worth considering also how to compose them. This brings up the whole question of constructing a language course. Before writing the first sentence of the very first dialogue, the author should draw up an inventory of all the linguistic items he proposes to teach. He should select the appropriate grammatical structures and the lexical items, on grounds of frequency, usefulness and productiveness. He should also take stock of possible causes of interference with the target language by the mother tongue. He should decide on the exact order in which he is going to grade and present the various problems. Then it remains for him to make up a list of topics and situations from real present-day life that will supply a natural starting point and setting for his dialogues.

Writing the dialogues themselves presents a special difficulty since there has to be a compromise between two diametrically opposite points of view. The linguistic content is decided by the writer, and it calls for a gradual advance along three fronts: phonological, grammatical, lexical. On the other hand, any real situation the writer may choose as his topic is bound to upset a grading built up on purely linguistical criteria. So the writer must try to avoid two major pitfalls: he must neither produce a series of dialogues that defy systematic grading, introducing too many words and too many structures too soon; nor must he offer the learner so-called conversations, expertly graded but quite artificial, made up of sentences that nobody would ever dream of uttering in the kind of situation he chooses as his subject. Finally, each dialogue must be all of a piece, with a proper beginning and end and without break in continuity, each remark or reply following on from what has just been said in a natural flow of conversation: in that way it will be all the more easily memorised. Lack of sense, of consistency or of logic should be taboo: they can only hinder the learning process.

So writing a language text-book is not easy. It requires high standards in these days if you are to produce really successful results. It is best done by a team, working together with the advice of linguists, of phoneticians, and of grammarians with a perfect knowledge of the two languages involved, and also relying on the spontaneous reactions of other native-speakers of the language taught. Of the two pitfalls mentioned in the previous paragraph, the danger of producing unnatural utterances is definitely the more serious, at least in my opinion — however much this might shock the 'structuralists'. Above all we must take care to teach language that is authentic. The old way of teaching living languages was too often at fault in that what was taught and insisted on in the schools was something quite different from what native speakers of the language actually said.

As one can see, the situation is by no means simple. In supporting the dialogue method, I have tried as far as possible to take the structuralist arguments into account, agreeing that the text-book writer should be guided by them, when he is both making up his dialogues and setting the relevant exercises. The method I am advocating has not yet been tested by scientifically-controlled experimentation. A thorough test, carried out under the control of psycho-linguists and educational psychologists is, I agree, necessary. None the less, the results so far obtained in actual teaching practice suggest that the disadvantages of the dialogue method are not nearly so formidable as the extreme structuralists feared. The high degree of motivation it arouses in the pupils would go a long way towards explaining the success it has enjoyed.

The real answer, as far as we can judge at the present time, seems to lie neither in extreme structuralism nor in a dialogue method that ignores both linguistic grading and pattern drill. It is more likely to be found in a judicious combination of the two, in something that could equally meet the demands of the linguists and the exigencies of educational psychology. This compromise has, in fact, been adopted in the kind of method developed in France and elsewhere in Europe in recent years. But the compromise has not taken stereotyped shape: far from it. It is undergoing constant change. At the present moment, for example, the method is being adapted to language laboratory techniques, particularly with a view to improving phonetic training and drills in grammatical structure. It is also being adapted to a certain amount of 'programming'[14]. For those reasons, it would be a pity to go into reverse and to abandon, for the sake of linguistic orthodoxy, everything that the use of a well-conceived dialogue method has done to make language teaching alive and really effective.

Chapter 4

Structural Drills: Theory and Practice

Having begun each step in the language learning process with a carefully constructed dialogue, Girard would then proceed to systematic practice of the structures that had been purposely introduced into the text. In the following chapter, he discusses the theory behind structural drills, pointing out that the notion of structure is central to many modern sciences, and has certainly been very important in linguistics and in language teaching. He also draws attention to the importance in foreign language teaching of systematic drill. He describes structural drills in detail, suggests how and when they might be used, and how the teacher could construct his own structural drills, to compensate for any weaknesses there may be in his text-book or to make more effective use of such equipment as a tape-recorder or a language laboratory as he may have at his disposal.

Enthusiasts for new methods of language teaching are often looked upon as followers of a new faith. Actually, what we believe in are certain basic principles, in facing linguistic facts, in considering the psychological and pedagogic implications of what we are about.

There is no dogma in structural drills. But there is a *theory* which we believe justifies their use, just as there is, in any science, a theory behind every application of that science. In this chapter, we shall consider the theory behind what are called structural drills, and see how it can be put into practice.

THE NOTION OF 'STRUCTURE'

'*Structural*' implies the existence of '*structure*'; and it is this notion of *structure* that I shall first try to explain, reminding the reader that it goes far beyond the bounds of linguistics and language didactics. It is, in fact, the central idea in every field of scientific development in the twentieth century. '*The notion of structure'* was the subject chosen for a conference in Paris in 1956 (organised by the International Centre of Syntheses), when scholars and research workers from all parts of the globe gathered together to define the structure of logical thought, the structure of mathematics, the structure of the new theory of physics, biological structure, psychological structure, the structure of the brain, social structures, and so on. The report of the proceedings filled 450 pages[1]. Linguistics was not represented at that gathering, which is surprising when you consider that we have been talking about *linguistic structure* ever since Ferdinand de Saussure at the beginning of this century. Linguistics opened the way for *structuralism* in the social sciences. However, although *Elements of Structural Syntax*, by Lucien Tesnière[2], was first drafted as early as 1934, it was not published till much later; and *structure* is not listed in the glossary of linguistic terminology drawn up by Marouzeau in 1951[3].

This strange omission was made good in 1959, when another international conference took place in Paris with *Structure* as its theme. This was the result of the compilation of a *Dictionary of the terminology of the social sciences*, under the auspices of UNESCO. This time, linguistics was worthily represented by Professor Emile Benvéniste, to whom we owe the first definition of *linguistic structure* and of *structuralism*:

> "Assuming that a language is a *system,* we then proceed
> to analyse its *structure.* Each system consists of items that
> operate on one another; and it is distinguished from other
> systems by *the internal ordering of these items: this internal
> ordering constitutes the structure*". (my italics – D.G.)

Another definition is contained in the following statement by Bastide:[4]

> "To regard a language (or each level of the language –
> phonological, morphological, and so on) as a *system
> controlled by a structure* that can be traced and described,
> is to adopt the 'structuralist' viewpoint".

That definition is very close to the one proposed, in 1948, by the great Danish linguist, Hjelmslev, and quoted by Professor Benvéniste:

"By *structural linguistics,* we refer to a group of studies
built up on the hypothesis that it is scientifically legitimate
to describe a language as being in essence an autonomous
body of internal inter-relationships, or, in a word, a
structure".[5]

We must however acknowledge that since Hjelmslev formulated that definition, the idea of *structure* in linguistics has
suffered a number of vicissitudes. Noam Chomsky, regarded as
the creator of transformational-generative grammar, built up *his*
theory in opposition to American structuralists, whom he criti-
cised for lacking a proper *theory* of language and for being
content with simply describing linguistic phenomena. Chomsky
developed a new conception of structure, in that he drew a
distinction between the *surface structure*, where structuralists
stop, and *deep structure*, on which *transformations* operate. It
is only in the deep structure that one can find the real clue to
the way in which a language works, and an explanation of the
extraordinary power of a child of five to 'generate' in his
mother tongue an infinite number of sentences that he has
never heard before[6].

If Alphonse Juilland[7] had been at the Paris conference on
Structure, he would no doubt have had something to say on the
multiplicity of meanings attached to the word, and on its
impreciseness. "Unfortunately," he writes, "as with most of the
basic terms in the empirical sciences, the meaning assigned to
structure and *structural* in linguistic studies is not very precise.
Like a number of other terms — such as *formal* (as used by
Bazell), *distributional* (by Harris), *functional* (by Uldall), *sub-
stitutional* (by Pike, Fries, Harris) and now *transformational* (by
Harris, Chomsky) etc. — which have sometimes constant, sometimes varying synonyms — the word 'structural' can be vague,
often ambiguous. *Structural linguistics* means different things
for different linguists; and, according to the context, its meaning may alter even in the writings of the same linguist."

STRUCTURE AND LANGUAGE TEACHING

So we have not made much progress yet in our efforts to
pin down the meaning of *structure* in its linguistic sense. That
shows us, incidentally, that it is not easy to 'do' *applied linguistics* in language teaching. With so much complexity and so
many differences of opinion before us, we should have to know

which linguistics we are trying to apply. But is that worth worrying about? Need the language teacher be involved in linguistic controversies? At least he must find out enough to be able to choose, from a variety of theories, the ones that will suit his purpose best. As far as he is concerned, the notion that *structure* is *an internal ordering of linguistic items* can be one of the most fruitful that linguistics can offer. It presupposes that what language teaching should be interested in is not the separate unit, the word, the syllable, the sound, but the functioning of linguistic *patterns* or *structures*. It is there that the real revolution in language teaching in our times has taken place, and not in the use of improved apparatus, however useful and effective ancillary aids might be. That revolution has of course been like every other one: it has not happened in a day. It has moved forward in a number of stages, which I would not have time to describe in detail now. If I might be allowed to over-simplify, I would say that the revolution in language teaching has progressed in three main stages. I will not attempt to give precise dates or draw clear dividing lines, because as in all such developments overlapping has been inevitable.

First – and this period lasted a long time – we taught *words*, often out of context. Learning a language was then a matter of acquiring a vocabulary, together with the *rules* according to which words could be put together.

Then we discovered the need for *context*; and that was the great merit of the Direct Method. But still, we must remember, although the word was embedded in a context, it was the word that mattered, whether we called it a 'lexical' (or 'content') or a 'grammatical' (or 'structural') word. The practice of printing new words in bold type was very significant. As for the grammar we taught, it was the grammar of *word categories*: the article, the pronoun, the possessive, the preposition, etc.

The third and last stage is that of structures: the *structure* replaced the word as the all-important item in our teaching. Teaching structures, the particular structures of the language being learnt, instead of teaching words, obliges us to deal with three main levels of the language: phonology, morphology, syntax. Let us take a few examples from the teaching of French:

On the phonological level, the interrogative in spoken French is often expressed simply by a change from the falling intonation of the declarative sentence to a rising intonation indicating a question. We must therefore teach the intonation pattern of a sentence fairly early on, in cases like *"Il est parti?"* (He's gone?), *"Ils sont venus?"* (They've arrived?), *"Elle est là?"* (She's there?), *"Vous irez?"* (You'll go?), *"Aujourd'hui?"* (Today?), where utterances which can be expressed in a variety of ways on the morphological and syntactical levels are identical on the phonological level in that the intonation pattern is the same in each case. Those sentences could be contrasted with sentences containing the same words in the same order, but having a different intonation pattern and thence a different meaning.

The notion of the *phonic word*, which is so important in the learning of the spoken language, is also closely linked to the notion of structure, in this case rhythmical and melodic structure. *Ils viendront chez nous l'été prochain avec leurs enfants* (They will come to our house next year, with their children) consists of ten 'words', from the written point of view. From the spoken, it consists of only three 'phonic words': *Ils-viendront-chez-nous / l'été-prochain / avec-leurs-enfants /*. This way of analysing the sentence is all the more important as it enables us, as well as making the right rhythmical and melodic divisions, to become aware of the *syntactical structure*, with its *nodes* and its hierarchy of 'dominances', explained by Tesnière[8].

Even the syllable can be usefully subjected to structural analysis. The frequency in a given language with which different syllabic structures occur, e.g. CVC (= Consonant-Vowel-Consonant), CV, CVCC, CCVC, etc, has its bearing on the teacher's work. A survey of such structures, with details of frequency of occurrence, has been made for certain languages. In the case of French, it is useful for the teacher to know that as many as 80 per cent of French syllables are 'open' i.e. ending in a vowel-sound (e.g. V, CV or CCV), even when writing obscures that fact. Thus, *"E/lle es/t a/llée/ /tra/va/iller/ a/ve/c u/ne a/mie"* (She has gone to work with a friend) consists entirely of 'open' syllables.

On the morphological level, the chief advantage of structural analysis from the teacher's point of view is that it makes a clear distinction between the morphological structures of the spoken language and those of the written. In French, gender, number, person and tense are expressed in quite different ways in the spoken and written systems. The morphological structure of the great majority of French verbs is far simpler in the spoken language than in the written. For example, *chanter* (sing), as well as *courir* (run), *croire* (believe) and *conclure* (conclude), each have only three forms in speech in the present tense as against five in writing[9].

The syntactic level is usually the one we have in mind when using the word *structures* in teaching. What we mean by *structure* in this sense is the patterning of elements, in this case the combination of words, in groups or *syntagmemes*, in phrases and in sentences. This is applying the notion of *structure* in a very restricted sense. But it is also true to say that the idea of structure in that sense is extremely productive in teaching. The syntactic structures which are apparent or concealed in the sentences we use are the raw material of our texts, whether spoken or written; and it is these structures that enable us to use the language for the purpose of communication. We have already noticed a close connection between phonological and syntactic structures. We can easily show that syntactic structure is not merely a matter of putting one word after another. The meaning of the sentence *Pierre travaille* (Peter is working) is not the sum of the meaning of each of the two words that make up that sentence: we must add the meaning contained in the syntactic relation between the noun, functioning as subject, and the verb. The syntactic structure accounts for an important part of the total meaning of the utterance; and it is probable that, in the development of a language, it preceded the emergence of individual lexical items.

Once we have agreed on the necessity of teaching the structures of a language – at those different levels – instead of concentrating on words, we have to decide which of a variety of pedagogic devices we shall use in teaching those structures. We can teach them in isolation, presenting each one in a series of sentences related to one another solely by the occurrence, in each one, of that isolated structure. That is, in essence, what the Americans called *pattern drill*. It is no doubt an advance on teaching isolated words. But, carried too far, pattern drill has the same defects as vocabulary learning. What is needed is to teach the structures, not in isolation, but in context, as is done in audio-visual or audio-lingual methods.

We then proceed in three stages: the learning of a dialogue so constructed as to focus attention on the structures we wish to teach; then exercises designed to enable the learner to assimilate the structures; and finally controlled oral work, based on the dialogue, and aimed at producing spontaneous expression, which should be the ultimate aim of all language teaching.

DEFINITION OF STRUCTURAL DRILLS

The theory, as well as the practical application, of structural exercises, was developed in America under the name of pattern practice or pattern drill. The term 'structural drill' was substituted later, so as to stress the connection with linguistic structure. The development of this kind of exercise corresponded with a growing need to make fuller use of available auditory aids — records, tape-recorders, language laboratories. At first, the teacher was content to make the pupils imitate exactly what they heard on the recording, and then to repeat it till they knew it by heart. This method was called 'mim-mem' (mimicry-memorisation); and what was learnt in this way was either a continuous text with sentences containing different structures, or a series of unconnected sentences all containing the same structure. It was soon found necessary to improve on this technique, isolating the various difficulties, dividing each one up into its main components, and then getting the learner to practise each structure intensively before proceeding to the next. At the same time, the boredom of sheer repetition was reduced by the introduction of a creative element in the pupil's role, so that he was no longer expected merely to imitate but also had to invent a sentence on his own, once he had grasped the underlying structure. Exercises of that kind were used first, and for quite a long time, as a means of mastering phonological structures[10]. Later, syntactic and morphological structures were practised in a similar way.

The first important study of the theory of structural drills was no doubt contained in the special issue of the *International Journal of American Linguistics* (Vol. 29, No. 2, April 1963), as a result of a conference on *Structural Drill and the Language Laboratory*[11]. Of particular interest in that publication are the articles by W. G. Moulton, S. Belasco and Earl Stevick. In the same year, B.E.L.C. undertook a team study of both the theory and practice of structural exercises. That resulted in the publication of two series of specimen exercises for use in the language laboratory[12], and in a booklet designed to explain the theory behind them, while explaining to teachers how they could make up similar exercises for themselves[13]. At about the same time there appeared a special issue of the journal *Le Français dans le Monde* devoted to structural exercises and written under the supervision of Professor Pierre Delattre, an eminent linguist and one of the pioneers of applied linguistics in the United States[14]. In the field of remedial phonetics, mention should be made of the two collections of exercises in French pronunciation worked out by Monique Léon[15]; while the University of Besançon produced a large battery of grammatical-structure exercises as an interim complement to the CREDIF course *Voix et Images de France*[16], until CREDIF itself could complete its own drill materials.

With the increase of language laboratories in France — especially in the universities and in the *Centres de Recherches et Documentation Pédagogiques* (the CRDP), numerous teams set to work preparing structural exercises for the teaching of French as a foreign language, and of English, German, Russian, Italian, even Latin. For English, excellent work is being done in the language laboratories in the universities, notably at Nancy, Strasbourg and Paris, thanks largely to the enterprise of Professor Culioli who for the last four or five years has organised an annual conference on laboratory work. Monsieur André Gauthier makes similar arrangements for the CRDP and has recently set us a very good example by publishing an excellent battery of exercises under the general title of "My friend Tony"[17]. It is worth noting, by the way, that Gauthier refuses to use the label 'structural drills'. He prefers 'Audio-oral structure practice'. This expression is not so compact, but it is a better definition of what he is trying to do. It has the advantage of bringing out a very important feature of structural drills, namely the fact that they *do* demand aural-oral practice; and it reminds us of the impossibility of forming sound and lasting linguistic habits through purely written exercises.

In this survey of what has been done in France over the last few years to develop this kind of exercise, I cannot of course fail to mention the steps taken by the General Inspectorate for Modern Languages which took the initiative in organising one-day courses to keep language teachers up to date with the latest developments in their subject. Topics have included audio-visual aids, the use of the tape-recorder in class, and structural exercises. This is a striking and very encouraging indication of the interest taken in these matters at the highest level in France.

After that rather long but incomplete historical survey, I

would like to describe structural exercises in greater detail, in order to show in what way they differ from other exercises used in a language class. I shall limit myself to three essential points:

1. emphasis on linguistic·structure, as we have defined it above;
2. the oral — or rather aural-oral — nature of these exercises;
3. the fact that they must follow a system.

EMPHASIS ON LINGUISTIC STRUCTURE

We decided to adopt Professor Benvéniste's definition of linguistic structure, namely *'internal ordering of items'*. Gap-filling exercises are not structural exercises in so far as they spot-light the *word* or the morphological element instead of bringing out the pattern or the combination of words. Consequently the learner is not made aware of the structure, and does not internalise it. Suppose we are teaching the French possessive adjective to foreign students. A gap-filling exercise will deal with the problem as follows:

C'est le livre de Pierre.	*C'est — livre.*
(This is Peter's book.	It's — book)
C'est la bicyclette de Paul.	*C'est — bicyclette.*
(This is Paul's bicycle.	It's — bicycle)
C'est la maison de nos voisins.	*C'est — maison.*
(This is our neighbours' house.	It's — house)

That kind of exercise stresses the grammatical *word: son* (his or her, before a masculine singular noun), *sa* (his or her, before a feminine singular noun) or *leur* (their, before masculine or feminine singular). To decide how to fill the gap, therefore, the pupil is required to perform quite a complicated mental operation, especially if, as in the case of English, his mother tongue uses the possessive adjective quite differently. In that operation, he must choose between *son, sa* and *ses* according to the gender and number of the object that is possessed, whatever the gender of the possessor. If the object possessed is *le livre* he must say *son livre*; if it is *la bicyclette*, it must be *sa bicyclette*. But then how will he account for the fact that with *la maison*, 'their house' = *leur maison?*

A structural exercise might take this form:

Model

C'est le livre de Pierre.	*C'est son livre.*
(This is Peter's book.	It's his book)

C'est le crayon de Jacques.   . . . .
    (pencil)

C'est le bureau de papa.   . . . .
    (office)

C'est le chapeau de M. Dupont.   . . . .
    (hat)   (Mr)

C'est le jardin de Mme Dupont.   . . . .
    (garden) (Mrs)

In that case the pupil must supply the whole structure, thus:

C'est son { livre / crayon / bureau / etc.

Such an exercise would only be the beginning of a *battery* of exercises in which one problem at a time — that is to say, *one* of the structural items — would be picked out and dealt with. The syntactic pattern remaining the same, the learner has more chance of internalising a variety of morphological-phonological structures that occur with the possessive adjective. In the exercise quoted above, for example, we are concerned only with the structure /sõ/ + C (= noun beginning with a consonant), when the noun referring to the possessor is singular.

With structural exercises, the learner does not find the right answer by carrying out a long process of reasoning. Beginning with imitation of the original model, he invents a correct sentence by fitting appropriate lexical items into the right slots in the syntactic frame. This becomes more and more automatic,

though it does not rule out the use of intelligence, as some
people are apt to believe. Intelligence and correct reasoning are
indeed required if the pupil is to find the analogy, to detect
the structure that underlies superficial differences. In any case,
the pupil's mind is soon freed from the problem of producing the
required structure, as it is when he is learning his mother
tongue; and it can then concentrate increasingly on the *meaning*
of the utterance, instead of being entirely absorbed by the
form.

With the conjugation of verbs, the traditional form of
exercise puts the emphasis on the verb-endings:

> je chanter**ai**   (I shall sing)
>
> tu chanter**as**   (you will sing)
>
> il chanter**a**   (he will sing)

Learning verbs in that way, the pupil fails to see the whole
morpho-syntactic structure and the extent to which the mere
verb-ending may be influenced by the sentence as a whole. On
the other hand, a structural exercise will bring out not only the
link between the person (first, second or third) and the inflection (between *je* and *-rai*, for example), but also the relation
between an adverbial of future time and the inflection that
marks the future, between *demain* (tomorrow) and *-rai*.

On this point, it is useful to remember Pierre Delattre's
definition of a structural exercise, since it sums up so well what
we have been saying about emphasis on a linguistic structure. It
is:

> "A structure is a succession of slots, and a structural
> exercise is a mechanism by which these slots can be
> systematically filled."

AURAL-ORAL PRACTICE

The form of a language that is most complete is its spoken
form, in so far as in it the three main levels (phonological,
morphological and syntactical) and the lexical elements are
most intimately inter-related. In the written language, the
phonological elements are represented very inadequately by the
graphic symbols and are often ignored altogether.

To return to the example of the possessive adjectives, it is
clear that a recital of the paradigm from the written language

(*mon, ton, son, notre, votre, leur, ma, ta, sa,* etc.) is only covering part of the total linguistic reality. The possessive *mon*, for example, has two pronunciations, /mõ/ before C and /mõn/ before V (not counting the variant /mon/); and it enters into three combinations:

	Masculine		**Feminine**
Before C	*Before V*	*Before V*	
/mõʃjɛ̃/ mon chien (my dog)	/mõn ami/ mon ami (my friend)	/mõn ami/ mon amie (my friend)	

On the other hand, if we consider not the 'graphic' word, but the 'phonic' word, which is the basic unit of the spoken language, we can make two further interesting statements:

1. In the phonic word, *c'est-mon-ami*, the possessive is an unstressed syllable, unless we wish to stress the reference to *my, not somebody else's*;

2. The normal rhythmic division of that phonic word produces four open syllables, /sɛ/ /mõ/ /na/ /mi/, in which case the nasal consonant /n/, occurring before V, becomes the initial consonant of the third syllable — it does not belong to the syllable that represents the possessive.

Neither of these two facts is reflected in the written form.

Structural drills do not teach a morphological or a syntactic structure by itself. They teach a complex structure in which the phonological, morphological and syntactic components are all present. On this point, too, we can refer to the undeniable authority of Pierre Delattre:

> "Language exercises cannot rightly be called 'structural' unless they are based on the phonological facts of the language, as revealed by the rigorous analysis of structural linguistics. That is the only kind of analysis that can account for all structural levels at once — phonetic, prosodic, morphological, syntactic and semantic".[18]

To that linguistic argument, we must add a *psychological* one. The perceptive-motor skills of hearing and articulation form the unconscious reflexes of speech, and they are much more potent in language learning than the act of writing is. Oral drill can impose a rhythm that we should do well to follow. In doing written exercises, the pupil takes his time over formulating a correct sentence which he would perhaps be unable to produce with the normal rhythm of speech. I am not suggesting that written exercises should be abandoned. They certainly have their place in language teaching. But they do not serve the same purpose as oral drills. Nothing can replace audio-oral practice as a way of ensuring that linguistic structures are firmly internalised.

STRUCTURAL DRILL MUST BE SYSTEMATIC

This is the third essential difference between structural exercises and the traditional kind. It is not by accident that the Americans use the word 'drill' in this context: the word 'exercise' has been weakened by over-use; and it does not have the same associations as 'drill' with military-type training. Learning to march in step or to present arms smartly involves much more than carrying out once or twice the actions required: they have to be performed dozens, even hundreds, of times. Notice the determination with which the young child repeats and repeats the fundamental structures of his mother tongue before he achieves a satisfactory degree of mastery in them.

Can we expect a foreign language to be acquired without the same sort of insistence? Every teacher of English as a foreign language knows that real command of the contrast between *since* and *for* — a bugbear for all French students of English — cannot be passed on simply by stating a plausible rule and by drawing a neat diagram, then setting one or two exercises on the strength of them. I have found a battery of fifteen carefully-graded structural exercises necessary before I can hammer that particular contrast home — and a battery of thirty-six before I could feel that the French possessives can be considered properly taught. In fact, as we have already seen, a grammatical problem is not a matter of *one* structure, but of a whole *complex* of structures, which may have to be driven in one by one, if we really want to follow Fries's advice and establish linguistic *habits*. That is why a mechanical aid should now be considered indispensable, whether it be a tape-recorder in the classroom or a language laboratory of one type or another. A mechanical aid can relieve the teacher of the tedious business of creating unconscious habits, and it is more effective as a means of establishing the regular rhythm of speech.

There are psychological reasons for carrying out structural exercises systematically. The concept of *linguistic behaviour* (associated with the name of Skinner[19]) is behind the idea of the four-phase drills specially devised for the two-track tape used for language laboratory work. The principle is this:

TEACHER'S track	stimulus		correct response	
STUDENT'S track		response		correct response repeated

The auditory impression of the correct response, coming immediately after the student's first answer, is what Skinner called the *reinforcement* essential for effective learning. In the traditional type of lesson, the teacher's approval served as a substitute for this reinforcement; reinforcement is one of the fundamental principles, and in programmed learning a battery of well-graded structural exercises can be one form of programmed instruction.

DIFFERENT TYPES OF STRUCTURAL DRILLS

Drills can be classified according to the *type of structure* that one is trying to teach. They can deal with:

    (a) phonological structures, either affecting the pronunciation of sounds, or suprasegmental features such as intonation, pitch, etc.;

    (b) morphological structures;

    (c) syntactic structures;

    (d) lexical features (although the lexicon hardly lends itself to structural treatment).

In reality, as we have seen, the different levels represented in that classification are closely linked together. The teacher often has to decide which level to concentrate on, and that will depend on what treatment his students need. It is sometimes necessary to deal with one particular level in revision or remedial work. That is what is done in language laboratories in French universities, when, for instance, special drills are devised for students handicapped by poor oral performance and needing remedial phonetic treatment. Similar work is done with pupils in the upper forms of secondary schools who need special attention to basic structures in grammar.

However, in every case, the levels are bound to be interlocked, although the exigencies of education may require us to concentrate on one or the other. The essential thing is to follow a strictly graded programme in treating our various problems.

To simplify again, we may pick out, as Pierre Delattre did, two main types of structural drill, corresponding to two fundamental linguistic phenomena — contrast (or polarity) and similarity:

"Applied to the teaching of languages, the notion of structure rests in the linguistic phenomena of contrast and similarity. Structural similarity enables us to construct substitution exercises, in which the slots remain the same and retain their special functions: we can replace a lexical item in one slot by another item of the same class[20] and this produces a change of *meaning*. Structural contrast, on the other hand, enables us to construct transformation exercises, in which a change in the nature or the position of at least one slot produces a different *function*".[21]

The two types of exercise, based on two opposing linguistic theories, provide an excellent illustration of the eclecticism which we can claim for 'linguistics applied to language teaching': we can borrow from each linguistic school whatever we find useful to our own discipline.

There is quite a number of catalogues of structural drills available now: those by Moulton, Belasco, Stevick, Lado, Mackey, Réquédat. . . . I think that one of the clearest and most comprehensive is by Mme Geneviève Delattre to be found in the special issue of *Le Français dans le Monde*[22] already mentioned. The reader may find it worth his while consulting her article, which covers the following kinds of exercise:

1. Repetition
2. Substitution:
   (a) simple
   (b) multiple
   (c) by expansion and reduction
   (d) involving correlation
3. Transformation
4. Expansion
5. Combination
6. Controlled dialogue:
   (a) contradiction
   (b) injunction
   (c) question and answer
7. Completion

Mme Delattre's classification has the added advantage of proceeding from the most mechanical exercises (simple repetition and substitution) to the freest (controlled dialogue, completion). The teacher thus has at his disposal a full range of drills that vary in difficulty, that impose a greater or lesser degree of restriction on the learner, that aims of course not at *imprisoning* the learner in a mesh of mechanisms but, on the contrary, at *setting him free* to express himself spontaneously and correctly. As Geneviève Delattre reminds us, "Beyond structural drills, there lies the vast, rich realm of spontaneous expression, oral and written."

PLACE OF STRUCTURAL DRILLS IN THE LANGUAGE CLASS

Structural drills are obviously very suitable for language laboratory work, whether one is using a simple audio-active laboratory, or one with separate booths and facilities for the student to record his own voice. In any case, the drills can be very easily used just with a tape-recorder. Does that mean it is impossible to use structural drills in an ordinary classroom, without any of this special equipment? I think not. On the contrary, it is in the teacher's interests to apply the underlying theories of structural drills at different points in his lesson, choosing the kind of drill that is most appropriate to a particular problem, to his text-book — and above all to the particular needs of the learner, which only the teacher can tell.

Please understand that I am not trying to maintain that structural drills are the alpha and omega of language teaching. There are plenty of other exercises, at least as important, that one can always resort to — for one, that spontaneous conversation with the pupils which is linguistic communication in its normal form and which is the best preparation for the natural use of the language. But these other exercises fall outside the bounds of this chapter. All I maintain here is that the linguistic and psychological principles behind structural drills can be profitably applied at every stage of language learning. I am thinking in particular of the four stages which — with variations, including variations in the actual or relative time taken over each stage — are the main sections of every well-planned language lesson, namely: testing *control* of what the pupils ought to know by oral questions on the previous lesson; *presentation* of new material; *application* of new material; *habituation or reinforcement*, with a view to making sure that new structures are properly grasped[23].

TESTING CONTROL OF MATERIAL ALREADY TAUGHT

This can normally be carried out by means of question-and-answer, one-way, teacher to pupil; in other words, by testing through oral interrogation. Generally the questions are on the notional content of the text studied, to see whether details of the story or of a description have been understood and remembered. In accordance with the theory of structural drills, we should put our questions in such a way as to make sure that the pupils can handle the structures in the text correctly; and this pre-supposes that a linguistic analysis of the text — phonological, grammatical, lexical — will have been made. Oral questioning is the most convenient form of review. But the form the questions take is important, and they should be graded; first, questions simply calling for the answer Yes or No; then questions containing the elements of the answer; and finally 'open-ended' questions, giving the student more and more freedom in his reply. However, there are other ways of checking, e.g. by substitution or transformation exercises, or by giving the pupil the answer and making him ask the corresponding question.

PRESENTATION OF NEW MATERIAL

This must be done as directly as possible, and with a double aim: comprehension of new items, and correct oral imitation. The most useful exercises at this stage are:

> (a) repetition: a whole phrase or sentence can be repeated; or, if the sentence is too long or especially difficult, it can be repeated by a process of 'backward building', starting with the *end* of the sentence and keeping the intonation pattern intact;
>
> (b) simple substitution, with just a few examples;
>
> (c) 'closed-type' questions, i.e. those requiring answers in which there is practically no scope for 'free' expression.

APPLICATION OF NEW MATERIAL

As this is best done by free conversation, it is the part of the lesson that least lends itself to structural drill. However, one can occasionally use substitution exercises at this stage, suggesting contexts that are similar to those of the lesson.

HABITUATION OR REINFORCEMENT

This is the really *grammatical* part of the lesson, whether a grammatical rule is stated or only suggested by a mass of examples. It is obviously at this point that structural drills can play their chief role. The basis of the drills should now no longer be the context but the *structures* themselves that have to be taught, though there is no reason for not using the actual words of the text as models. The aim should be to ensure that the pupils know, memorise and retain the most important structures in the text, and can use them automatically, before going on to the next lesson. That requires a three-fold teaching procedure:

> (a) presenting every time a clear and correct model as the basis for a series of exercises;
>
> (b) adopting an order of presentation, graded according to difficulty;
>
> (c) developing a fluent rhythm in the mechanical mastery of the structures.

For such procedures, one should be able to draw on the whole range of structural drills in one's inventory, though it may not be necessary to use them all. This part of the lesson will naturally take time. It is not time wasted. Indeed, it would be wrong to cut this part of the lesson short on the grounds that a limited time-table does not allow you to spend much time over it — and that the text-book has to be 'done' by the end of the school year. One of the merits of audio-visual methods is certainly that they oblige the teacher to devote a long enough period to reinforcement for it to have proper effect; and a high degree of effectiveness can be ensured by proper use of the tape-recorder.

Structural drills that are necessarily of a mechanical type should not be such as to bore the students. Boredom is the mortal enemy of pedagogic efficiency. It is essential to vary the way the drills are presented; and the same drill can be presented in any number of disguises. For example, you could start with a picture (slide, film strip, or a picture on a flannel board) when you are dealing with a drill on structures used in description, so as to bring in the following:

FRENCH		ENGLISH	
il y a	un, une, du, de la	there is there are	a, some, no
il n'y a pas	de l', des, de	there isn't there aren't	any

with transformations from one structure to another. *Visual presentation* is always very welcome with younger pupils, and it introduces an element of relief with older ones. Instead of a picture projected on to a screen, built up on the flannel board or drawn on the blackboard, you could sometimes use real objects; and a scenic game is always very effective. Presented in that way, the structural drill loses a lot of its abstractness and its association with mental gymnastics: you bring it right back to the realities of living language.

Alternatively, you can present the same drill purely *orally*, with or without mechanical aids. This is no doubt the best way when there is no problem over understanding the lexis, and when it is only a matter of properly assimilating the structure.

With a language laboratory at your disposal, you can perhaps begin the exercise in class, where the teacher is freer to direct and control the pupils' reactions, and carry on with it in the laboratory with more effect and fewer chances of mistakes.

After that, you can go on to *written presentation with oral reaction*, reinforced by written exercises; these will not be the old exercises with a catch in them, but will provide real opportunity for enriching the pupils' language, especially as the oral preparation in itself will have considerably reduced the chances of error. *Substitution tables*, as used nowadays in class, are an excellent means of written presentation. There is the foolproof table that allows every possible combination; or, if you prefer, the table which obliges the pupil to make a semantic choice and a structural one at the same time, and to take care that the result is both sensible and grammatically acceptable. Here is an example in French:

		oiseau rossignol hirondelle oiseaux nid feuilles		la l' le	branche buisson arbre haie mur	au- dessus près à côté	de des de la de l' du	fleurs rivière maison roses route eau pont
Est-ce qu'il y a	un une des		sur					

Or in English:

		bird nightingale swallow birds nest leaves			branch bush tree hedge wall	over near by		flowers river house roses road water bridge
Is there Are there	a any		on	the			the	

A table like this, which can 'generate' dozens of correct sentences, gives ample scope, in French, for driving home the interrogative structure (*est-ce qu'il y a*), the three forms of the indefinite article (*un, une, des*) and of the definite article (*le, la, l'*), the contracted article (*du*), and prepositions of place followed by *de* etc. It is an extremely useful table for revision.

If we agree that structural drills are a pedagogic instrument usable at certain stages of the lesson, and especially at the stage where grammatical structures are being firmly established, then every language teacher ought to be capable of making up his own batteries of drills to compensate for whatever gaps there may be in his text-book and, should it be necessary, to make fuller use of his tape-recorder or the language laboratory.

What I shall do now is suggest a few ideas for constructing the drills I have tried to describe. For more detailed guidance, I would refer the reader to the book by François Réquédat[24]. Here, I shall simply mention six or seven basic principles, following the order in which the relevant operations should take place.

1. *Choose the structure(s)* that you want to teach: e.g. the use of *since* and *for* in English; in French, the possessives, the use of *il faut* (one must), the personal pronoun as object, the present perfect, etc.

2. *Make a list of the difficulties*, taking into account both a comparison with the pupils' L1 and the phonological difficulties inherent in the L2. It is easy to anticipate the troubles that English-speaking learners will have in dealing with the French possessive adjectives, e.g.

   (a) agreement with the noun referring to the thing possessed, not with the noun referring to the possessor;

   (b) agreement according to gender and number, plus the case of *mon amie*;

   (c) difficulties in the spoken language (/mõ/ and /mõn/) which necessitate drills containing nouns beginning with a consonant, then with a vowel.

3. *Work out the order* in which these difficulties will be dealt with, thus:

   (a) *le (crayon) – mon (crayon),*

   (b) *la (bicyclette) – ma (bicyclette),*

   (c) *le* or *la – mon* or *ma* (+ consonant),

   (d) *mon/ma – le, la,*

   (e) /mõ/ + consonant, /mõn/ + vowel,

(f) *mes* with masculine and feminine plural, but with
two phonological forms, i.e. /me/ + C, /mez/ + V,

(g) 1st, 2nd and 3rd persons singular, etc.

4. *Work out likewise a suitable order for the drills you
propose*, starting with the simplest and most mechanical, and working towards the more sophisticated. For
example: repetition, simple substitution, substitution
with two changes, transposition, transformation.

5. *Work out an internal order within each drill*, selecting
what you want from a large number of sentences, retaining only the ten or twelve most suitable, and avoiding as
far as possible sentences that are artificial or of little
practical use, such as *Mon tailleur est riche* (My tailor is
rich), *La plume de ma tante est dans le jardin* (My aunt's
pen is in the garden) or *Est-ce que les chats sont verts?*
(Are cats green?)

6. *If you record your drills*, take great care to see that the
intonation patterns are perfectly natural. If you are
drilling the possessive adjective, for example, do not give
it unnatural stress.

7. *Vary your method of presentation* so as to avoid monotony. Decide how long each drill, each set of drills and
each drill-period should be according to your pupils'
capacity to concentrate on this kind of work and to
take it all in.

SUMMARY

1. The *theory* of structural drills is based on:

(a) the scientific notion of *structure*;

(b) *purely linguistic applications* of that notion;

(c) *psychological principles*, such as the need to divide a
problem into its elements, to form habits and
unconscious reactions, to provide reinforcement of
new material, etc.

(d) *pedagogic principles*, such as the importance of
proceeding from simple to complex; of avoiding a

surfeit of the same thing and especially avoiding excess and monotony in drilling; of not over-tiring the learner, etc.

2. From the teacher, the *practice* of structural drills demands considerable study and understanding of the theories behind them, as well as careful, patient training.

3. There is much more in these drills than a mere *teaching technique.* In any case, a mere technique cannot provide a solution to all the teacher's problems.

4. In their proper place, drills of this kind are more than a passing fashion. They can make a very positive contribution to the language lesson at all levels, including the university, as increasing experience in language laboratories in French universities has shown. They form only one part of the whole strategy of language teaching, but they undoubtedly provide one of the most effective means of increasing productivity in the small but none the less exceedingly important field of effective foreign language learning.

Our conclusions in fact coincide precisely with those of Mme Delattre who summed up the advantages and the limitations of structural drills very well in these words:

"Structural drills are only a means to an end, but I think an effective means — so long as one realises their possibilities and their limitations — of training students to think within the grammatical framework of a foreign language, *without interference by their mother tongue.* They facilitate the forming of new linguistic habits which eventually become second nature, so that the speaker or writer can give all his attention to communicating his ideas instead of being distracted by the mechanism of expression. The restraints, often very strict, under which the pupil is held during a course of structural drills, and the concentration on one problem at a time, with a model to imitate and with control over the accuracy of the imitation, ensure that the development of bad linguistic habits can be kept to a minimum. The different types of drills I have described are useful tools. They have no magic power. Nor do they offer any new solution to the greatest problem of

all in language learning — how to create motivation when it
does not exist already. Their value will therefore depend to
a large extent on how they are used and on a clear
understanding on the part of the teacher of their purpose
and their limitations".

Chapter 5

Language and Literature

The general question of methodology includes the particular question of what kind of language to teach. Traditionally, teachers assumed that the student should be led as soon as possible to the language of literary classics. There has been a strong reaction against this assumption during the last few decades – not nearly strong enough, perhaps, among conservative teachers or in over-optimistic official programmes, but too strong, no doubt, in the practice of zealous believers in the virtues of commonplace colloquialism. In this chapter, Girard points out that literary expression is not only one form of culture among others, but it is also one of many forms of language. The chapter ends with a chart which illustrates the variety of forms a language may take. While fully aware of the importance of literature, he puts it into what he considers to be its rightful place in the curriculum, maintaining that a sound knowledge of the fundamentals of the present-day language should come first and that literary studies should start with contemporary texts.

The conflict between the traditional view of modern language teaching, which regarded the foreign literature as all important, and the current view, which is focused on the effective use of the language as spoken and written today, has created what might be called the 'lang.-lit. dichotomy'. Like many apparently insoluble problems, it is not really a problem at all. A literature is only one – admittedly often the most important – of the many facets of the cultural heritage of a language community. We would do well to examine, objectively and dispassionately, the relationship between a language and the culture of which it is a part[1]. Such an examination would entail reference to the real aims of teaching a language. We might adopt the principle – as official educational programmes generally do – that the teaching of a language should not be an end in itself. It should be, as it were, a path along which the learner can be led towards the discovery of a culture of which the language is perhaps the most privileged but certainly not the sole medium of expression.

A language has a double function, in that it is an instrument of *communication* between members of the same linguistic community, and a *cultural medium* in a wide sense which covers, among other things, literary expression.

1

The function of language as a means of communication has been stressed by practically every linguist for the last fifty years. If I may repeat and expand a quotation used earlier in this book, André Martinet called a language "an arbitrary system of phonic symbols which meets the need for communication within a human community." Linguists speak of a *code* which makes possible the transmission of concepts in a two-way operation of encoding and decoding with the aid of a system of signals and symbols. In most languages, this code is two-fold in another sense: it has an oral system, using phonic symbols, and a written one which is by no means an exact representation of the other. In French, for example, such categories as gender and number may be marked quite differently in the two systems, as we can see from an analysis of these two sentences:

	ORAL SYSTEM	WRITTEN SYSTEM
Singular	ləptitãfãsamyz	le petit enfant s'amuse (the little child is amusing itself)
Plural	leptizãfãsamyz	les petits enfants s'amusent (the little children are amusing themselves)
	(2 phonic symbols changed, i.e. ə > e, t > z)	(5 written symbols added)

(a) *The language as an instrument of oral communication* is sometimes realised in *monologue*, as in sermons, speeches, lectures, papers read at conferences, etc.; but it then operates only as one-way communication, thus:

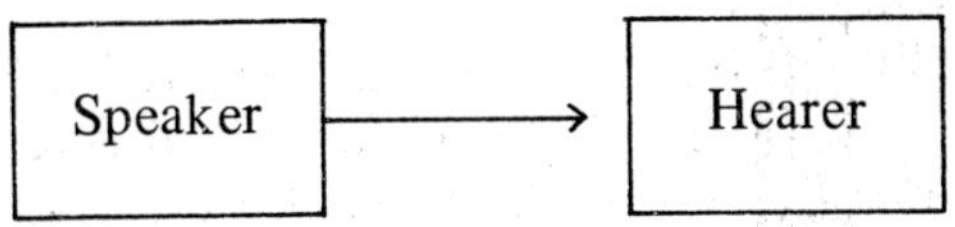

It is mostly realised in *dialogue*, in conversation involving two or more voices; and this accounts for the greatest and most widespread use of any living language, since it is shared by everybody in the linguistic community, of whatever degree of general intellectual and cultural development. This kind of communication is *two-way*:

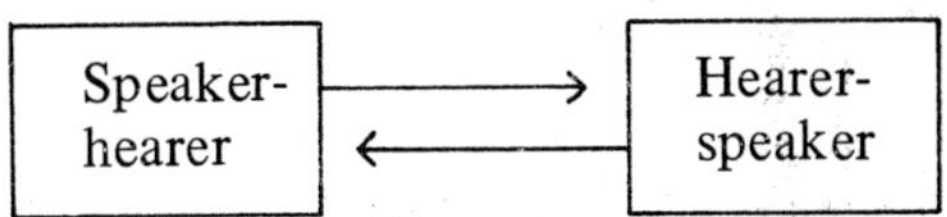

Every contemporary expert in language teaching (including the teaching of the mother tongue) would agree that language learning should begin with *oral communication* as the basis of all linguistic usage. That is why we now normally begin the teaching of a foreign language by presenting to the pupil *dialogues* which can be easily imitated and which reflect exchanges frequently heard in everyday life.

(b) *The language as a complete instrument of written communication*, producing communication two ways, is practically only found in familiar correspondence which acts as a kind of written dialogue:

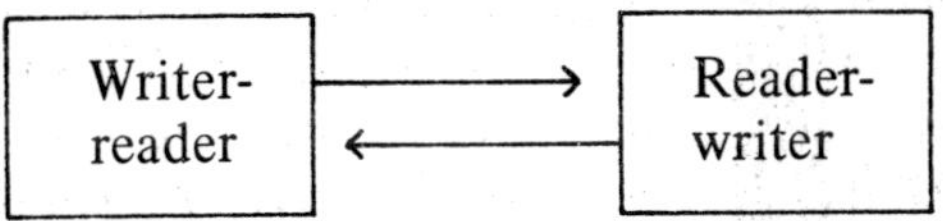

This form of communication occurs in limited sections of the linguistic community and only in certain situations, e.g. when near relatives and intimate friends are separated.

On the other hand, one-way written communication is exceedingly common in every literate sector of the community. It occurs in written messages of all kinds: posters, pamphlets, prospectuses, programmes, bills, order forms, announcements, newspaper articles, and so on.

From the teaching point of view it might only occasionally be possible to make profitable use of these different forms of written communication. In any case, the teacher would not come to them until fairly late, and he would generally initiate his students into the written language through transcriptions of oral dialogue, bearing in mind the differences, already noted, between the two systems.

2

THE LANGUAGE AS A CULTURAL MEDIUM

So far, we have not touched on the *content* of the messages exchanged orally or in writing. We have only indicated the kind of context in which the primary function of language, i.e. the instrument of *communication*, operates. Let us now consider the pre-eminent role of language as a *cultural medium*.

However, before doing so we must at once admit that language is not the only cultural medium. The culture of a nation can be seen first of all in the attitudes and behaviour of its members, in the way they have fought their battles or turned nature to their advantage, in their development of techniques and in their scientific progress. That is the practical and material side of culture, the outcome of trial and error and of the people's intelligence. There is also the more disinterested side that is concerned with making life more agreeable and lifting men out of their material preoccupations. That takes us into the realm of the arts, and of spiritual, religious and metaphysical values. There, the role of language is, beyond doubt, supremely important, especially as language and thought are closely related – at least, so psychologists and linguistic philosophers tell us. But the plastic arts, music and dance have little to do with language, though in some countries they are manifestations of untold cultural wealth. These latter media of artistic expression are also means of communication, no doubt less precise but often subtler than language.

Where does literature come into all of this? It is one of the facets of this many-sided culture. Thanks to the invention of the printing-press and to the expansion of scholarship, it has reached out to a wider and wider public and has become perhaps the most popular of the cultural media. But it must be remembered that in medieval Europe the populace found its stories and its poetry expressed in the stone carvings over the doorways and on the pillars of cathedrals.

Yet, if in recent centuries the development of written literature has been spectacular, literature in oral form has enjoyed a revival in our own times; and it has always been the only form in many countries, as in the tales of Barbary and in the oral literature of Africa.

The place occupied by *literature* in the *use of language as a cultural medium* can be shown in the following table:

Language as a cultural medium	oral	linguistic content (every linguistic system is, of itself, a manifestation of the culture of a community)
		oral communications with cultural content (scientific, technical, moral, religious, etc.)
		purely oral literature (tales, legends, ballads, songs, etc.)
		written literature presented orally (as in poetry and drama)
		works composed for radio or television
		artistic creations for the cinema
	written	the press, and press reporting — aiming at providing *information*
		scientific and technical papers and articles — aiming at providing *information*
		critical studies — concerned with *aesthetic expression*
		written literature in all its forms — concerned with *aesthetic expression*

From that table, it is easy to see that literature, in its narrow sense, does not cover the whole of language, as many text-book writers seem to have assumed. They have supposed that as soon as the fundamentals of the language have been taught, usually in the first two years, there is nothing else to do but proceed to an anthology of literary texts, generally presented in chronological order. Such an idea immediately brings us to another subject, very important from the teaching point of view, namely that of the *varieties* of a language.

3

VARIETIES OF A LANGUAGE

We have already discussed two varieties — the *spoken language* and the *written*. We could also refer to them as two *modes* of expression which correspond, as we have seen, to two quite different *codes*.

But there are numerous other varieties that can be clearly distinguished by linguistic analysis. In normal language usage, whether it is for purposes of communication or for cultural expression, we only in fact employ a very limited part of an immense linguistic potential. The part we select depends on our role as speaker or writer, on where we are, on our place on the social scale, on our particular purposes at the time of speaking or writing, and on the nature and the size of our audience.

Thus we can distinguish the following other varieties:

- *historical forms of a language:* every language undergoes a process of evolution, and it changes from age to age. The language of Shakespeare is not that of John Osborne, nor the language of Montaigne that of Albert Camus.

- *social levels of language*, from the most vulgar to the most refined. Thus, a language will differ according to the social environment to which speakers and hearers happen to belong or in which they happen to be at the time.

- *dialects*, i.e. varieties of the language which differ — phonetically, grammatically and in word usage — according to the region in which it is spoken.

- *registers*, i.e. forms of the language which vary with the content and purpose of the communication. We may therefore find technical, scientific, administrative, political, military, literary, religious and other registers.

- *idiolects:* an idiolect is a form of language bearing the peculiar, indelible imprint of the individual speaker or writer.

- *styles*, i.e. forms of the language which are used by a speaker or writer when he is expressing himself in a certain way — conversationally, formally, artistically and so on.

Traditional language teachers have paid insufficient attention to these variations in their raw material. If it is true that we never use more than part of a language, it follows that we can never expect to *teach* more than part of it. We must therefore decide what part or parts we are going to teach, and we should base our decision on definite criteria.

The introduction of literature into a school course should only take place after the most careful consideration of the varieties of language this will involve. It also requires full awareness of the fact that the literary use of a language entails one-way communication only, namely:

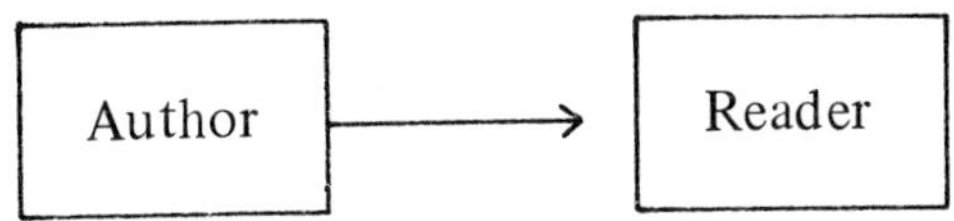

It is not through the study of literary texts that the student can learn to handle language as an instrument of communication, any more than he can use language written for artistic purposes as a model to imitate when he simply wishes to convey plain facts. A literary text is interesting in so far as it reflects the author's original *style*, which is his *own* and is therefore by definition inimitable. The study of literary texts is very important for the development of the student's aesthetic sense and taste, and as a way to a deeper appreciation of the culture concerned. But how is it that some of us still fail to see that it is not the way to practical communication, and that it presupposes a perfect command, on the part of the student, of the common core of the language, which the author adapts, distorts and transforms for his own artistic ends?

4

PLACE OF LITERATURE IN THE TEACHING OF A LANGUAGE

Bearing in mind what we have just been discussing, we may now try to work out a scheme that would put literature in its rightful place in the teaching programme and would show how it is related to other forms of the oral and written language. In doing that, we might conveniently divide our students into three groups — Beginners, Intermediate and Advanced. I shall not specify how long the course for each group should be, beyond suggesting a period of two or three years according to differing timetables.

BEGINNERS

1st Stage: command of the basic current spoken language. This would come, in my view, as a result of the kind of work on everyday dialogue that I have suggested elsewhere in this book.

2nd Stage: command of the basic current written language, through:

(a) transcriptions of the dialogues;

(b) narrative texts, especially written according to strict structural grading;

(c) suitable extracts from newspapers;

(d) extracts from contemporary writers, adapted to the students' linguistic level.

It goes without saying that at the second stage the text only serves as a basis for the lesson, which will always be primarily oral.

INTERMEDIATE

3rd Stage: introduction to contemporary literature through authentic extracts, chosen in accordance with clear criteria, and especially with a view to facilitating the transition from everyday language to the language of contemporary letters[2].

It is at this point, when we start the transition, that we begin introducing literature into the language class. We shall incidentally be upsetting an old custom, and deliberately reversing the sacrosanct chronological order by which authors used to be introduced. Formerly one started with authors who used the historical form of the language farthest removed from that of contemporary communication.

At the beginners' and intermediate levels, learning should be

active. The student is trying to master a new means of communication in order to equip himself to explore a foreign
culture; and all our teaching effort should be directed towards
helping him gain that mastery. All the material we present
should be a *model*, whether it consists of dialogues, concocted
texts, extracts from newspapers or passages from authors.
Exercises that involve a reconstruction of texts of that kind are
much more productive, at these levels, than literary comment or
the traditional textual analysis[3].

ADVANCED

4th Stage: initiation step by step into other levels of the
language and other registers. This will include a
study of the facts of the foreign civilisation, through
texts specially selected.

5th Stage: progressive initiation into the *historical forms* of the
language, working backwards chronologically, with
texts selected according to:

(a) their linguistic content;

(b) their cultural content;

(c) their literary merit.

It is not until we reach this fifth stage that we can be
content, though not always then, with a *passive* knowledge. The
main object is to *comprehend*, in the full sense of the word – to
comprehend authors of the rank of Racine, Corneille or
Voltaire, to appreciate them, to enjoy them, but not to try to
imitate them.

Comprehension will be all the more effective if the work at
the preceding stages has been done thoroughly. Of course, the
students will always be coming across new words and constructions that they must not only understand but can also add to
their own active knowledge, thereby increasing their linguistic
repertoire and acquiring a richer and more polished mode of
expression, both spoken and written.

That is how, as I see it, literature should gradually be integrated into the work of learning a language – without becoming
an end in itself, which is the concern of specialists in literature
and in literary criticism.

SUMMARY

The teaching programme I have advocated could be sum-marised in the form of six principles which I think should always be followed:

1. We should give priority to the *oral* language at every level. Even at the most advanced stages, we should accustom our students to listening to a text and discussing it, with their books closed.

2. We should give priority to language as *communication*, oral then written.

3. Texts should be chosen for their *linguistic content* as much as for their cultural and artistic value.

4. Texts should also be selected with a view to their *audience appeal*, and according to the age and background of the students.

5. The *exploitation* of the texts should be carried out in stages, such as:

   (a) *elucidation*, concentrating on the linguistic content;

   (b) *appropriation*, by the students, of important new linguistic items, by the type of application and habituation exercises described in Chapter Six.

   (c) finally, *appreciation*, which need not always be explicit: an expressive reading of a text is by itself an excellent way of helping the students to *feel* it, although they may not be able to explain their feelings.

6. *Study in depth* of short extracts should alternate with *more extensive reading of set passages*, the latter being followed by oral and written summaries, with a view to developing a taste for private reading and to improving the students' written composition.

Literature is not the whole of culture. It is an important element in it. Language is a part of culture: it is first of all an instrument of communication, and our first task as teachers is to enable our students to handle that instrument. After that, the way is open: they can systematically explore all the rich cultural territory that the language leads them to, and enjoy all the literature to which the language holds the key.

LANGUAGE AND LITERATURE

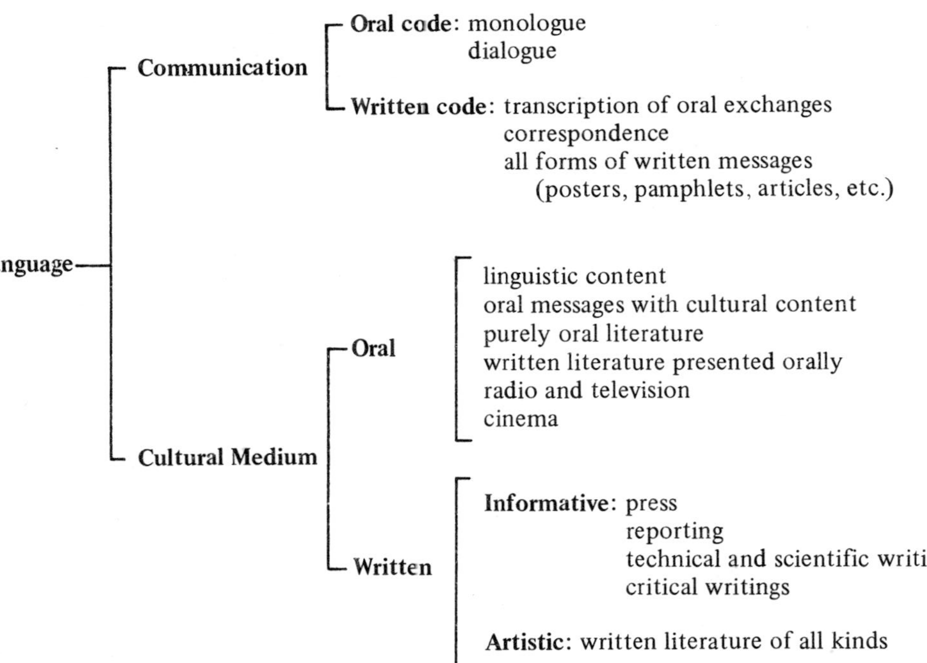

Varieties of language

1. *Modes:* oral
written

2. *Historical forms*

3. *Levels,* according to
social environment and
particular situations

4. *Regional dialects*

5. *Registers* (technical,
scientific, etc.)

6. *Idiolects* (with
personal idiosyncracies)

7. *Styles,* according to
aim, which might be:
expressive
artistic

Part 2
PEDAGOGY

Chapter 6

The Four Phases of the Language Lesson

The following chapter suggests how exactly a language lesson might be planned and conducted. The author expresses the view that, whether one is teaching beginners or at any other level, the lesson should proceed in four stages which he explains in detail, with practical examples of the kind of work that can be done at each stage. The author's original examples were taken from the teaching of French as a foreign language. In rendering those examples into English, I have tried to show that Denis Girard's principles and procedures can be applied to English equally well.

Imagine you are giving a foreign language lesson. The pupils have been learning by the Direct Method, by which I mean that they have not been taught *via* the mother tongue. What I want to do in this chapter is to suggest techniques that could be generally applied, whatever the text-book you have to use. Let us assume you are following a method based on principles of modern linguistics applied to language teaching and aimed at the best possible command of the fundamentals of the L.2. The class you have to teach is, say, one you might find in any good average secondary school offering a basic two or three year course in the foreign language.

We shall try to work out what your aims should be, to analyse the means you might employ, and describe in some detail the procedure you might adopt. I could take my illustrations from one particular level — the beginners', for example, and suggest drills that could be used, step by step, on the basis of a given text. But I prefer to illustrate my points with examples from different levels, from the first year to the third or fourth, to show that the procedure I propose is valid throughout the course, provided you are careful to adapt the theory, the rhythm and the rate of progress to the standard of your students.

D

In the normal conditions under which secondary schools are at present organised, the time factor is all important: the teacher has an average of only about a hundred periods during the school year for each class. He is therefore compelled to ration his time with the utmost economy, spacing out each activity as wisely as he can. Ideally, then, the language lesson must be used as a kind of precision instrument.

Most modern language lessons, whatever the method, the text-book or the teaching equipment available, should generally be conducted on the four parts mentioned in Chapter Four (pages 63-64).

1. a quick **check, revision** or **review** of what the pupils ought to know. This, more often than not, is done at the beginning of the period; and it has the double purpose of

   (a) turning the pupils' attention to the subject, preparing them mentally for what is to come, and

   (b) letting the teacher judge how well the previous lesson has sunk in.

2. **presentation** of new material with concentration on its form, its meaning, and the relation between the two;

3. **application** of the new material, setting it to work immediately in oral interchange, and applying it in the context of what the pupils have already learnt;

4. **reinforcement** – fixing the new grammatical structures firmly in the pupil's mind, so that he can handle them correctly and fluently.

No doubt all trained teachers prepare their lessons with those four phases in view, and with exercises to match. However, it is possible that not all of them have a very clear idea of the difference between one step and the next, or of a precise object at each stage. In particular, many teachers are uncertain of how best to divide up their time or of what are the best techniques for each of the four phases.

FIRST PHASE: CHECKING AND VERIFYING WHAT SHOULD HAVE BEEN LEARNT

Every language teacher would consider himself a good judge of what progress his own pupils have made. Yet a very common fault is to limit testing to only one aspect of the previous material, namely the vocabulary. One teacher may be satisfied if he receives, as a reply to his question, a particular word, with no context and pronounced in such a way as to be unrecognisable by a native speaker of the language. In that case, all such a reply shows is that the pupil has remembered one of the dozen or so new words learnt last time. Another teacher may be concerned only with the logical content of the previous text, not with the linguistic content; and he will give a generous mark to the pupil who can reproduce the main ideas of the story, or better still describe one of the characters in it, or even comment on the aesthetic merit of the passage, even if all of this is expressed ungrammatically and, as far as the natural language is concerned, almost unintelligibly. How can we convince such teachers that that kind of thing – so often done and blessed by magisterial encouragement – can in fact do more harm than good, even when the most glaring of the pupil's mistakes are corrected as he stumbles along? Is that a real linguistic test of the previous lesson and a useful preparation for what is to follow? What I would call a real check would be in one way less ambitious, in another way more so: less, in so far as we ought only to be testing one thing at a time, and by means of a limited number of questions; more, in so far as we should be insisting on phonetic and grammatical accuracy, not simply on reproducing isolated lexical items.

We must not forget, either, that all we are doing at this stage is testing: we should not waste time on long monologues, in which we imagine we are 'explaining', and which will make very little impression now.

As an example of the procedure I would recommend, let us take an extract from *The Fall* by Albert Camus, set for a third year class:

"An Autumn Evening in Paris

It was a fine autumn evening, still warm over the city already damp on the Seine. Night was approaching, the sky was still clear in the west, but darkening; the street lamps

were shining feebly. I was walking up the left bank towards
the Pont des Arts. The river could be seen glistening in the
gaps between the closed quayside stalls. There were few
people about on the embankment: Paris was already dining.
Under my feet, the yellow, dusty leaves were reminders of
the summer. The sky was gradually filling up with stars, and
I could see them, fleetingly, as I moved away from the light
of one street lamp towards the next. I relished the
returning silence, the evening softness, the empty city.
I was content."

That passage is predominantly descriptive and the narrative
element is minimal. The teacher who wanted merely to make
sure that the general content and the chief facts of the extract
were known, would ask questions like this:

What city are we in?

What season is it?

What time of the day is it?

Were there a lot of people on the quayside?

Were there any stars in the sky?

Was the hero content?

The answers to such questions would be necessarily very brief,
and the pupils could slide easily out of most of the linguistic
difficulties. The conscientious teacher, on the other hand,
would have made a list of these difficulties — the use of the past
continuous (*was approaching*), the contrast between *still* and
already, between *still clear* and *darkening*, the use of the im-
personal passive *could be seen*, of *few people*, of the adverbs
feebly and *fleetingly*, and so on.

He would then have picked out those items which were
within the range of his class, and decided how the passage could
best have been exploited linguistically. He will therefore know
which items it would be fair to test, and which are matters of
style (e.g. the use of the adverb *fleetingly*) and therefore more
suitable for study at a later date. Finally, he will have put his
questions or his test exercises in a suitable order, that is to say,
the order of increasing difficulty. With that extract from
Camus, the test could take some such form as this:

<table>
<thead>
<tr><th>TEACHER</th><th>PUPILS</th></tr>
</thead>
</table>

1. Was it an autumn evening or a summer evening?

   (The question contains the reply, which requires no transformation)

   It was an autumn evening

2. Was the sky getting dark?

   Yes, it **was** (getting dark)

3. Give me a sentence using one word instead of 'getting dark'

   The sky was darkening

   (Simple transformation, testing a new lexical item)

4. Where was the speaker?

   He was in Paris
   He was on the embank-
   ment beside the Seine
   He was on the left bank of
   the river

   (Pupils should be prompted to give more and more precise answers so as to lead on to the next question)

5. Where was he going?

   He was walking up the
   left bank towards the Pont
   des Arts.

To be able to answer those questions accurately, the pupils must obviously have learnt the text almost by heart. That is an ideal rarely achieved by everybody in the class. But the best pupils can, by their example, help the weaker ones along; and if that kind of test is well done, proceeding from the simple to the more complex, it can help the weaker ones to remember the text quite satisfactorily. It will naturally have helped if the right kind of exercise had been done on the text in the previous lesson.

The example of teacher-pupil dialogue given above belongs almost entirely to the question-and-answer type of exercise. It starts with very simple questions containing the elements of the reply, and ends with questions that require the student to make a more and more complex reconstruction of part of the passage. It includes an example of a simple transformation which calls for a comparatively uncommon expression (*darkening*) which

none the less is worth knowing, as it illustrates an important
feature of the language (compare *weak, weaken, strength,
strengthen*). Other kinds of transformation can be used to make
sure that syntactical constructions occurring in the text have
been mastered. This, by the way, is why I prefer to speak about
checking or verifying what should be known rather than vaguely
'asking questions on what was done last time'. The checking
might continue as follows:

TEACHER	PUPILS
6. "There were few people on the embankment". Replace the word 'few' without changing the meaning.	There were not many people on the embankment
7. Repeat that last sentence using *boats* and *river*	There were not many boats on the river
8. Now using *cars* and *streets*	There were not many cars on the streets

You should not forget the reverse of the question-answer
exercise — the very useful one that expects the pupil to think of
a question that would produce a given reply. Thus:

TEACHER	PUPILS
9. The *river* could be seen	What could be seen (glistening) (in the gaps between the closed stalls)?
10. It was filling up with *stars*	What was the sky filling up with?
11. No, gradually	Was the sky filling up with stars quickly?
12. As he moved away from the light of one street lamp towards the next	When did the speaker see the stars?

As you see, this type of check departs from the traditional
way of discussing a text. Does this mean that questions on style,
on the particular colouring of the text, or on its literary merits,
should be ruled out? Certainly not. But one thing at a time.

Introducing texts by contemporary authors into a language lesson, you cannot help beginning to initiate your students into the language of literature and an appreciation of literary works; and that will later call for special techniques. Real initiation into literature can only take place when the fundamentals of the language have been presented and thoroughly assimilated: it cannot replace thorough study of the linguistic fundamentals, even at an advanced level. Trying to carry out two entirely separate operations at once — language study and literary appreciation — traditional teaching too often ended up by failing to achieve either.

SECOND PHASE: PRESENTATION OF NEW MATERIAL

After various checks of that kind — and remember they must be done quickly, like warming up exercises in a gymnasium — you start on the new lesson. The first part of the new lesson, which I have called 'presentation', takes up an excessive proportion of the time in classes which it has been my responsibility to inspect. I must perhaps clear up a misunderstanding over that word *presentation*. It is of course the teacher's business to 'present' what is new in a lesson, drawing attention to the *form* of the new items (phonetic, morphological, syntactic, and, after a certain point, orthographic), at the same time making sure the pupils understand the meaning in the given socio-cultural context. However, that does not require a continuous monologue from the teacher, while the pupils sit listening passively to the master's voice. That one-sided manner of presentation is fortunately becoming less and less fashionable. It may perhaps do something to increase the pupils' capacity for aural comprehension; but, as for their oral expression, it usually provokes no more than the acquiescent monosyllabic "Yes" in reply to the question "Is that clear?" with which the teacher occasionally interrupts his own discourse. I shall confine myself to an analysis of 'presentation by dialogue' that invites constant and active participation by the pupils.

This part of the lesson must be quite short. The teacher must resist the temptation to devote to it the major part of the time at his disposal, to the detriment of the remaining sections. He must aim at two things: making sure

(a) that the meaning of the new text is understood, and

(b) that the new linguistic models are repeated correctly.

To that end, a strict economy of means must be practised; no matter what form the presentation may take, or what level one is dealing with, or what may be the composition and size of the class, the teacher's temperament, the technical equipment at his disposal, whether he is using visual or auditory aids, whether he is in an ordinary classroom or a language laboratory, etc. — it makes no difference: *presentation must be quick and effective.* In any case, explanations, given in the L2, must be very short and must be followed at once by examples of the newly-taught forms in action. Those examples should be repeated, individually and collectively in turn, while the teacher pays careful attention to the phonetic quality of the reproduction of the model. As models for repetition, you should always start with the phonic group, which is generally not only the phonic unit but also the semantic and syntagmatic unit at the same time, and which is the main thing to concentrate on when you are trying to create automatic habits in the spoken language.

For example, in French, the complex group *Il est allé à la poste* (He has gone to the post-office) should be apprehended and mastered as one uninterrupted utterance — with its *liaisons*, without any break between the vowel sounds, with its two rhythmic stresses and its intonation contour — before any attempt is made to analyse it. The word — and this applies even more to the syllable or the phoneme — must only be isolated in the very exceptional circumstances in which it might be desirable to emphasise a contrast with other items in the L2 or perhaps in the L1. When this *is* necessary, then the word, syllable or sound that has been picked out should immediately be put back into the group and repeated in its full context. To ensure understanding of these phonic groups, you should always put them in the context of a real situation, avoiding any abstract dictionary-type definition which isolates the concept and takes it out of its place in the normal stream of speech. One concrete, well-chosen example is much better than the best of definitions. You could use multiple contexts, e.g. *Le monsieur traverse la rue* (The gentleman is crossing the street), *Une balle lui a traversé la jambe* (A bullet has gone through his leg), *Une idée m'a traversé l'esprit* (An idea has crossed my mind), and make use of every available medium of visual representation — slides projected on to a screen, photographs, flannel board, blackboard drawings, gesture or mime. The teacher must be aware of all these possibilities and be prepared to use them to

92

good effect. Visual aids provide a short cut from the concept to its spontaneous expression in a foreign language lesson. They cut out recourse to the mother tongue which, from the very beginning, is nothing but a hindrance to progress and a strong inhibiting factor. Repetition of a good model of the spoken text, whether the model be the teacher's own voice or a voice recorded on a record or tape, should be a real activity that absorbs the attention of the pupils all the time and stimulates their creative instincts. The repetition should never be merely passive and mechanical.

Carried out in that way, the presentation should be a definite step towards command by the pupils of key points in the language from which they can then advance in the next phase: that advance will be directed towards the exploitation of their new gains.

As an example of presentation at the beginning of a first-year lesson, let us look at the first part of the sketch in Unit No. 20 of the *French Course for Cambodia*, prepared by B.E.L.C. under the direction of Jean Bertrand:

> LY: Daddy, may I have some money, please?
>
> MR KHEM: Some money! Who for? For yourself?
>
> LY: No, it's for Mummy.
>
> MR KHEM: What for?
>
> LY: To buy some tea, some fruit and some meat.
>
> MR KHEM: Here you are! I'm giving you two francs.
> Where are you going?
> To the market?
>
> LY: No, I'm going to the grocer's and to the butcher's.
>
> MR KHEM: Wait! I haven't got any cigarettes, Buy some cigarettes for me too.

In the first part of the presentation, either the teacher reads the dialogue clearly but with normal conversational rhythm and intonation, or the pupils listen to the dialogue played back on a tape-recorder. The pupils' books are closed. The auditory impression is reinforced by a visual aid (in this case, a set of movable figures on a flannel board) which goes a long way towards making the meaning of the dialogue clear even before the teacher begins any explanation. In any case, the teacher has already made a note, in the Teacher's Book, of the most important items in the text, some of which have been taught before. They include:

Structures

Who for? What for?

To buy some tea, some fruit, some meat.

I'm giving you. . . .

I haven't got any. . . .

Lexis

buy, grocer's, butcher's.

Difficult sounds

final *t, v*, etc.

Intonations

exclamatory, interrogative.

What the teacher has to do is to see that the pupils understand and absorb the new grammatical, lexical and phonological items as soon as possible, with the minimum of intervention by himself and with the class actively participating. To that end, he will go over the dialogue sentence by sentence, like this:

TEACHER	PUPILS
Daddy, may I have some money, please? Repeat, all together.	Daddy, may I have some money, please?
X, ask Y for some money.	Y, may I have some money, please? *(Two pupils act this little scene)*
Some money! Who for? For yourself? Repeat: Some money!	Some money! *(Insist on correct intonation)*
Z, ask me for some money.	Sir, may I have some money, please?

Some money! Who for? For yourself? *(With gestures and mime)* Repeat.	Some money! Who for? For yourself? *(Insist on the two different interrogative intonations contrasted with the exclamatory)*
Who for? For Ly? Repeat.	Who for? For Ly?
No, it's for Mummy. Repeat.	No, it's for Mummy.
X, is it for Ly?	No, it's for Mummy.
What for? To buy some tea. Repeat.	What for? To buy some tea. *(Insist on the two contrasting intonations)*
I'm buying a book. *(The teacher goes through the motions of buying a book from a pupil)*	
Give me some money to buy a book. Repeat.	Give me some money to buy a book.
Y, ask me for some money.	Sir, may I have some money, please?
What for?	To buy a book.

Thus the lesson goes on, without any theoretical explanation, but with, alternately, repetition pure and simple (in chorus and individually), and an exchange of questions and answers which are very similar to those of the original dialogue but which give the pupil a chance of intuitively understanding the exact meaning of a word or expression in a precise context. The pupil is therefore able to absorb the new word or expression, and add it at once to his active knowledge of the new language.

In the 'presentation' phase, then, the aims are that the pupil should as soon as possible acquire an adequate understanding of the content of the lesson as a whole; be able to repeat each phonic group correctly; and know the dialogue or text perfectly. This phase is most important, as the effectiveness of the rest of the process will depend on the quality of the work done at the start. However, it is, after all, only a start.

THIRD PHASE: APPLICATION OF NEW STRUCTURES AND LEXIS

From that beginning, the next step will follow naturally. This will involve the application of the linguistic items that have just been learnt; or, better still, an exploitation of them. By that I mean putting them to use in contexts slightly different from the one in which they were introduced, though close enough to it for the new items to come easily to the pupils' minds. There is a sound reason for recommending that this exploitation should immediately follow the initial presentation and should precede the stage of habituation when the aim will be to establish the principal new structures as habits through the construction of series of grammatically acceptable sentences. The reason is that the presentation and exploitation stages have the common factor of starting from a real context or situation, the only difference being that at the first of these two stages the situation is new to the pupils and outside their personal experience, whereas at the second the teacher uses all his ingenuity to suggest situations that are already familiar: in this way the pupils will be induced to express themselves freely. So now it is a matter of breaking down the barrier erected through learning the dialogue or text by heart. That was a good way of starting; but it was no more than that. The 'learning by heart' technique, as with most audio-visual devices, is effective but restrictive: and once it has had its effect, you should break away from it quickly. Otherwise, there is a danger of keeping the pupils bound by the automatic reactions triggered off by the visual stimulus, but associated only with that stimulus and with the situation it represents. Their reactions and expressions will then be stereotyped and they will find it difficult to express themselves easily and spontaneously in new contexts. The all-important aim of the exploitation stage is to enable them to convert the new linguistic material into 'their own words', adding it to their previous active knowledge and learning to use it consciously.

Experience has shown that to get the best results at the exploitation stage you must follow certain rules carefully. First, you must be on your guard not to start teaching more new material; not to let yourself be side-tracked in the course of conversation into making up lists of associated words, or quoting the various comparisons and contrasts into which the grammatical structures you are teaching can enter. Remember, you are now not teaching new linguistic items; you are trying to get the pupils to use correctly the items you have just finished introducing to them. By the same token, you should not spend much time correcting pronunciation and grammar: corrections may be necessary, but they should now be made quickly, without explanatory comment, and with an immediate return to the work of exploitation. The idea of that is to avoid breaking the spontaneity of the main exercise. Another important rule is to see that oral interchange at this stage continues with a rapid rhythm. Obviously this would be impossible if the teacher could not refrain from constant interruptions in his anxiety to go on teaching and correcting. Above all, the pupils must be given confidence and must not be inhibited by untimely interventions. A further point: in preparing what he proposes to do by way of exploitation, the teacher will already have in mind, without the pupils knowing, the habituation exercises that will come at the next stage. He will therefore contrive to make the pupils use, in their exploitation, the most important of the structures that he proposes to drive home later. The difficulty is to do this quite naturally. You must avoid artificial contrivances as far as you possibly can if you really want the learner to succeed in using the language for his own ends, expressing his own ideas in it spontaneously.

The exploitation, therefore, should proceed step by step, as every good teaching procedure should, from the simple to the complex, from the relatively artificial to the freest expression. The first step should be simple repetition, as in the presentation stage. If you are using a dialogue, you could make a group of students act the dialogue, identifying themselves with the characters in it and picking up their cues naturally. Then suddenly you could introduce slight variations without changing the structures, but giving the pupils an opportunity of using the structures for something they want to say. For example, let us look back at the lesson from the *Course for Cambodia*. Among the devices used at the presentation stage in that lesson were some that went beyond simple repetition and were already enticing the learner towards an original application of the new items: for instance, the scene where the teacher asks for money to buy a book and then invites one of the pupils to imitate him.

At that point in the lesson the object was only to make sure
that the meaning of the question "What for?" and the answer
"To buy a . . . ." was understood and absorbed in the context
of that situation. That object has now been reached. What you
should be doing in the exploitation part of the lesson is getting
the pupils to use the new structures again, not in *one* context
but in several similar contexts. The new situations could first be
those that can be created in class. You could get all the class to
participate in building up a dialogue exactly on the model of
the original which they will by now have learnt. Thus:

> JOHN: Jack, may I have some money please?
> (Or, as a variation, "may I borrow" instead of
> "may I have".)
>
> JACK: Some money! What for? For yourself?
>
> JOHN: No, it's for my brother.
> (Possible additions: "He hasn't got any money",
> "Nor have I".)
>
> JACK: What for?
>
> JOHN: To buy an exercise book.

Then you could switch to an imaginary situation: someone
wants to buy tobacco for Father, some sweets for a little sister,
some chocolates for Grandmother, etc., etc. In that way you
could bring in as much as possible of what the class has already
learnt, letting it be a natural part of the dialogue and making
this controlled conversation so much the richer. The new dialogue thus compiled by collective effort could sometimes be
learnt as the original one had been, if it is good enough and
lends itself well to dramatisation.

There are a number of pedagogical procedures that the
teacher can use so as to intervene discreetly in what is going on,
without being more than a ringleader in this process of impro-
visation. Having suggested a subject, or having described a
situation, he can give one or two precise instructions e.g. "X,
ask Y to do so-and-so. Tell him so-and-so. Do so-and-so and
then tell us what you are doing"; and then he could let the class
get on with it. That, incidentally, obliges the pupils to make the
transformation back from indirect speech to direct, itself a very
useful language exercise. For this kind of activity, the class
could be divided into two groups asking each other questions.

The brighter pupils in each group would stimulate the weaker ones; and the teacher would be able to ensure that the latter at least had an opportunity of repeating good sentences. However, it is more important to encourage exchanges with or between individual pupils, calling on them by name, and stimulating a personal response related to real experiences.

It is understood that the teacher will not fail to use any ancillary aid that could support this exploitation exercise — actual objects, pictures, photographs, puppets, flannel board figures, transparencies, and film strips (which can be full of ideas). Neither should he neglect opportunities, later on, to refer to the news of the day, to well-known happenings, to any events that may have fired the pupils' imagination and aroused their interests, for this will increase their motivation. Everything is grist to your mill so long as the mill turns merrily, and so long as the pupils get into the habit of expressing themselves in the foreign language and doing so with enjoyment.

Often, such aids are unnecessary: a good text and the pupils' own imaginations can produce all the exploitation you need. I found this true when I was dealing recently with a class of Italian pupils in their second year of French. The class was doing a short extract, from Robbe-Grillet's *Snapshots*, entitled "The Beach". The presentation had been done with the help of a simple sketch on the blackboard and a few brief explanations. We had managed to achieve a good oral reconstruction of the extract, in the course of which all the main linguistic items I had picked out for treatment had been mastered, before the pupils had so much as seen the text. After the class had spent a short time reading it, I suggested a topic for exploitation: "Imagine two children walking along a deserted street in an Italian town in July". A very lively conversation was built up on that slender basis, each one contributing something to its construction. A new story was invented on the model of "The Beach". I was surprised when next day some of the pupils brought me a short written version of the story they had composed orally. You will see below the text of one of these pieces of homework, side by side with the original extract by Robbe-Grillet: from it, you will notice that the disciple had obviously followed the master very faithfully. Other pupils had strayed farther from the original and had shown more originality. But clearly the principal object had been accomplished: those students had adopted for their own purposes the linguistic features of the model text, not only in the oral work we had done in class but also in the written application done at home. That is what I call 'exploitation'.

The Beach

Three children are walking along a seashore. They walk on, side by side, holding hands. They are all about the same height, and no doubt the same age too — about twelve. The one in the middle, however, is a little smaller than the others.

Except for these three children, the long beach is completely deserted. It is a fairly wide strip of sand, with an even surface, devoid of rocks or of pools, sloping up almost imperceptibly from the sea to the steep cliffs that seem to offer no way out to the land.

It is very warm. The sun's rays beat down violently, almost vertically on to the sand. There are no clouds in the sky. There is not a breath of wind either. The water is blue, calm, without the slightest ripple coming in, although the beach is on the open sea that stretches away to the horizon.

The Deserted Street

Two children are walking along a street. They walk on, side by side, holding hands. They are both about the same height, and no doubt the same age too — about ten. The one walking near the wall, however, is a little smaller than the other.

Except for these two children, the long street is deserted: there are no people and no cars. It is more a lane than a street, not too wide, straight, with an even surface, devoid of pavements and of shops, and sloping down almost imperceptibly from one end to the other.

It is very warm. The sun's rays beat down violently, almost vertically, on to the grey surface of the road. There are no clouds in the sky. There is no sound in the lane either. In a little basin attached to the wall, the water is clear, without the slightest ripple. The air is very hot, although the lane opens at each end on to two small squares. The children walk on, side by side, holding hands.

FOURTH PHASE: REINFORCEMENT OF THE NEW
MATERIAL

Many teachers imagine that their work is done when they
have presented the new lesson and succeeded in getting the
pupils to apply its main constructions. A common error is to
spend too much time on the presentation, so that the rest of the
lesson suffers; but few teachers accustomed to the Direct
Method fail nowadays to get through the presentation and
application phases somehow. The same cannot be said of the
reinforcement phase, which is often reduced to a rapid theoretical explanation (very much like the old 'grammar lesson')
and to a few purely formal exercises which the pupils are
usually expected to finish at home, entirely on their own.

Even though your presentation and your application may be
as lively, as precise and as systematic as I have suggested they
should be, that is not enough. It is no guarantee of definite
assimilation, of lasting acquisition of real linguistic habits. In
the traditional type of language learning, there is a great deal of
wastage. A lot is taught, and the immediate results, the performance of pupils who 'know the lesson they had today', may be
impressive. But do they remember it? Far too much is in fact
forgotten; and knowledge that appears to have been learnt
simply because it has been once 'understood' tends to melt
away like snow in the sunshine: the reflexes associated with
audition and expression, the basic mechanisms, have not been
firmly established. That is why this next phase in the lesson —
the phase of *reinforcement* or *habituation* — is of prime importance and should have our full and very careful attention.

Here again, there are principles that must be observed. First,
we must realise that the procedure will be different from the
one which we have followed so far and which always meant
starting from a context — given in the presentation phase,
chosen freely in the application. What must now decide the
content of the exercises are the forms and structures that have
been extracted from the context because of their importance to
the fabric of the language. As with the checking and presentation phases, you should begin by making up a list of items to
be dealt with. However, the list now will be shorter, since you
should not try to include everything in the reinforcement phase.
You must make a judicious choice depending on what your
students have already mastered and on the productiveness of
the new forms, their frequency and general usefulness.

From that point of view, let us look again at the extract from Robbe-Grillet. In the second or third year of study, there are certain items in the text that you can omit without hesitation, as items that need not go beyond the limits of the pupils' passive knowledge. To understand those items in their context is quite sufficient, and it would be unreasonable to expect the pupils to be able to use these actively yet. Such items might include the lexical ones *ripple, devoid,* and *imperceptibly*; and the construction *devoid of rocks.* However, that is for the teacher to decide in the light of his assessment of the pupils' knowledge and capacities. What he *should* include in his list for drilling are such items as *along a (line), walk (go, come) on, side by side, about the same height (length, width, weight), in the middle, smaller than, the others, there are no . . .,* etc.

The exercises you will now be doing will be structural drills of various types in which lexical items will of course occur. The drills should always be done in sets and with quite a fast rhythm so as to produce automatic fluency. The pupils ought to be able to 'generate' a score of sentences in four or five minutes. For this purpose, you could use every type of structural drill: substitution, transformation, expansion, question and answer, analogy, opposition and so on[1].

While they are trying out the potential semantic productivity of this or that structure or syntactic frame, by means of substitution and other exercises, the pupils should gradually become aware of the notion of structure. They would then much more easily understand certain explanations, in terms of grammatical theory, that would have to be given to them eventually.

How exactly habituation exercises are conducted will depend on the material and equipment at your command. A tape-recorder in the classroom is invaluable and you should always be able to use it to good effect[2]. Those who are fortunate enough to have a language laboratory in their school can use it to complement exercises begun in the classroom. But there is no need at all for the teacher who has none of this equipment to leave the habituation exercises out. They can always be done without special apparatus.

Whatever technique you adopt, it is essential to follow a systematic order in the drills you choose, otherwise you will run the risk of discouraging the weaker pupils and of letting only the brighter ones gain any benefit.

May I give you an example from exercises I used to drill important items occurring in that extract by Robbe-Grillet? Remember the idea in this phase is not to stick to the text and to the order in which certain items are found in it, but to work from the simplest exercise to the most difficult.

SUBSTITUTIONS

1. **It is very warm.**

    Change *warm* to *hot, cold, wet, windy, mild,* etc.
    (The pupils themselves found these substitutes.)

2. **Three children are walking along a seashore.**

    (a) Change *seashore* to *beach, road, street, lane, path, railway line.*

    (b) Change *walking* to *running, going, coming, dancing, hopping.*

    (c) Change *children* to *men, women, boys, girls, people, soldiers.*

You can ring the changes as much as you like, provided you keep the structural word *along* and the idea of moving along a line.

SIMPLE SUBSTITUTIONS IN TWO PARALLEL CONSTRUCTIONS

1. *There are no (clouds in the sky). There is not a (breath of wind) either.*

Make up ten pairs of sentences on the same pattern:

There are no children in the street. There is not a car either.

There is no chalk in the room. There is not a duster either.

2. *The water is calm, without the slightest ripple.*

Use *without the slightest* in other sentences:

The village was quiet, without the slightest sound.

The road was straight, without the slightest bend.

The journey was easy, without the slightest difficulty.

This last exercise is obviously harder than the others because it involves substituting whole clauses and not merely separate nouns or verbs.

TRANSFORMATION

1. Replace *three* by *two* in the first paragraph, and make the other changes that will then be necessary *(all-both, in the middle-on the right (or left), the others-the other)*.

2. Begin the first sentence with *yesterday*. Then read the whole text in the Past Tense.

I am sure you could think up other exercises dealing with other structural problems arising out of that extract. What is important is to allow enough time for such exercises, and to vary the ways you present them — by games and competitions according to the age of your class, by substitution tables on the blackboard, by structures put up on the flannel board, and so on. On the other hand, you have the responsibility of seeing that the exercises are strictly limited to the structures you have chosen to drill. Within that framework, the pupils themselves should be allowed a considerable degree of freedom and should be encouraged to bring in as much of their existing knowledge of the language as possible.

Those, to my mind, are the essential parts of a language lesson, each having a precise aim. That does not mean that other activities need be excluded. At the right time, the beginnings of literary criticism, textual analysis, explanations in detail, translation within reason, will all have their place, for students who reach the required level. But I am convinced that even at the most advanced level, the modern language lesson must be first of all a lesson in the *language*, aimed at building up linguistic competence and performance; and that this is the first condition for proceeding towards literary and artistic appreciation. Certainly, the kind of study I have outlined in this chapter should be the groundwork of the first three years of foreign language learning.

What I have called 'the four phases' of a language lesson could correspond with four parts of the same period, though it is neither possible nor desirable to specify how many minutes should be spent on each part. The four phases could also be spread over more than one period, in which case the teacher would have to decide at what point to break off and how to keep the duration of each phase in its due proportion. The teacher's art consists very largely in knowing how to time, space out and vary his pedagogical techniques; in not taking too long, or in taking long enough, over his various activities; in impressing his own personality on the class; in remaining in all circumstances an operator — a manipulator in a complicated and exciting game — who knows exactly what he is doing.

Part 3

TEACHER TRAINING

Chapter 7

The Training and Further Training
of Modern Language Teachers

Chapter Seven sets out the author's views on the type of basic training, and the continual re-training, that are required for the kind of language teaching that is being more and more widely attempted today. As he has had considerable responsibility for organising training courses in France, as well as courses for the teaching of French in other countries, it is, as he says, not entirely a coincidence that the syllabus for some of those courses should resemble the training programme which he believes should be more generally adopted in the future.

The chapter is based on a talk given at the 9th Congress of the International Federation of Modern Language Teachers at Uppsala, Sweden, August 1965, when the author took the opportunity of reminding teachers' associations that much of the initiative for developing improved forms of training depends on the teachers' associations themselves.

"When a man teaches something he does not know to somebody else who has no aptitude for learning it and gives him a certificate of proficiency, the latter has completed the education of a gentleman."

G. B. Shaw, in the Preface of *Man and Superman*

THE ROLE OF THE TEACHER

If, thank goodness, teaching only rarely resembles the caricature that Bernard Shaw drew of it, the great British humorist called our attention at any rate to three of the chief factors that play a part in all pedagogy, namely the qualifications of the teacher, the aptitude of the pupil and the nature of the final examination that supposedly assesses the results achieved in relation to those aimed at. That clearly raises the question of what we are trying to teach and what we are aiming at.

To complete the picture, we might add one more factor: the method and the teaching material used.

In the way it is put to us by Bernard Shaw, that satirical definition of teaching suffices to unleash indignant protestations from the right-minded teachers that we are. The teaching profession has been too often slandered for us to accept such an accusation without a word. It would be easy for us, indeed, to demonstrate that the failures that occur in education in general — not only in language teaching — are typical of the modern world and are due to the complete disparity between increasingly difficult working conditions — overcrowded classes, inadequate timetables, out-of-date syllabuses, and crash-training of teachers — and the ever-growing demands of a hyper-technical civilisation which expects people to have the maximum of knowledge in every subject. However, it is in the teaching of living languages that weaknesses in education are most striking and give rise to most speculation. It is therefore worth while considering why this should be.

If, out of the four factors mentioned a few moments ago, I have chosen the teacher as the subject of this chapter, it is for two fundamental reasons. First, everyone would agree that the teacher is an essential element in the success or failure of an educational programme. We all know that a good teacher who has received first-class training is capable of overcoming every obstacle presented by the pupils, the curriculum and the teaching material, though that does not mean that it is unnecessary to take any action to improve his general conditions of work. The second reason for my choice is more personal. It happens to have been my duty, for a number of years, to train teachers of language — of English in Morocco, and of French in several other countries. Since I have been with B.E.L.C., dealing with the teaching of French throughout the world, I have been concerned with summer courses for teachers, and B.E.L.C. in the last five or six years has organised courses for hundreds of teachers from over fifty different countries. That is why I am interested in the further training of teachers as well as in their initial training, and why I propose to deal with both aspects of the subject. The problem of further or in-service training, of re-orientation, would not be so acute if the initial training given in the universities were more satisfactory and bore a closer relation to present-day needs. I am thinking particularly of the situation that we now have in France and in most of the countries where I have been appointed to serve. An enquiry into the unsuitability of basic teaching training might profitably be undertaken by the *Fédération Internationale de Professeurs de Langues Vivantes* (FIPLV: the International Federation of Modern Language Teachers).

I must add that this problem of the basic training of language teachers, directly affecting as it does the question of their further training, is of such concern to us at B.E.L.C. that we organised a conference on the subject in Paris, in 1964, with the support of the Council of Europe. I would like to refer to the provisional conclusions which emerged from that conference and which helped certain national bodies – certainly the Modern Language Teachers Association in France – to present specific recommendations to their respective authorities.

The line I propose to take here is to start with a brief analysis of the basic training for language teachers as it now is in most countries, looking at its positive side as well as its defects; to proceed to an account of what the ideal form of training might be; and then to consider the possible steps that might lead towards that ideal. This will oblige us to consider how the task of further training in its various aspects might be undertaken, and how the most glaring gaps might be filled, until the trouble can be treated at the roots, that is to say at the basic training level.

INITIAL TRAINING OF LANGUAGE TEACHERS

We must consider this aspect of the matter under three headings, corresponding to the three divisions into which public education generally falls, although where the dividing lines actually run may vary considerably from one country to another. I refer to:

1. the primary or elementary level;
2. the secondary (whether grammar, modern or technical);
3. the university.

I shall not deal with the training of university teachers, which is effected through personal research work and usually depends on some previous teacher training and teaching experience. It is in fact this previous teacher training that I am most concerned with, and it is usually part of the general training for work in the secondary schools.

At the primary level, the teaching of foreign languages is, in the main, something quite new. The most spectacular developments in this field have undoubtedly taken place in the United States, with the rapid expansion of the Foreign Language in Elementary Schools (FLES) Program; and in Great Britain, where the Department of Education and Science and the local education authorities have started intensive courses as a result of a conclusive experiment carried out at Leeds a few years ago. However, there have been interesting experiments in other European countries too – in Italy, for example, and more recently in France. The problem is different in Africa, where what for the pupils is a foreign language has to be used for purposes of general communication; and that applies even in countries where the language – English or French – is considered as a national one. That is an enormous problem which merits special study on its own. One need only mention Congo-Kinshasa, where, according to reliable sources of information, out of 50,000 teachers only a few hundred are up to the standard of the French ordinary school-leaving examination, held after no more than four years of secondary schooling.

As a general rule, it is safe to say that the training given to teachers of foreign languages at the primary level is minimal. There is a strong tendency to rely for such teachers either on native speakers of the language who have had no professional training at all, or on good teachers fired with enthusiasm and the best intentions. The latter are usually given a short refresher course in the language, and in the use of the teaching material, which they are expected to stick to closely. At best, this material includes recorded models and a detailed teacher's manual. With this equipment, they are expected to inculcate a command of the fundamental structures of the spoken language. The aims of instruction at this stage are, rightly, limited to elementary conversation, and to arousing interest in the foreign language and the countries where it is spoken.

Training in the proper sense is non-existent. Everything depends on how good a man or woman may be as a teacher, on personal enthusiasm, on the adequacy of the material the teacher is supplied with, on the keenness of young children and on their capacity for language learning. However, it is worth drawing attention to the remarkable progress made by the Department of Education and Science in Britain in organising courses for teachers of French in primary schools. These courses provide for three months' linguistic training in France, followed by instruction in methodology in the home country. Mention should also be made of the two-year course organised by the authorities in Sweden.

At the level of secondary education, a distinction should be made between what might be called the *normal training* for qualified secondary school teachers and what I would call the *short-course training*, which is only a stop-gap in an emergency and which makes it possible for us to use willing teachers for duties that they are not properly trained to undertake.

By *normal training*, I mean training at university level recognised by the award of a university degree (B.A., *licence*, or the equivalent), and completed by training in pedagogy. This would, according to the degree of specialisation attained, cover several kinds of professional training given at the end of three or four years of compulsory university studies. One such kind of special training is given, for example, in England at an Institute of Education or in a university department specialising in the teaching of English as a foreign language. In France, it is given in a course, leading to a competitive examination for the CAPES (*Certificat d'Aptitude au Professorat de l'Enseignement Secondaire*) or to the *Agrégation*. This requires specialisation in teaching practice or in literature.

Germany provides us with a good example of thorough training in two distinct parts: four or five years study of the language and civilisation at a university, followed by two years of compulsory professional training in a *Studienseminar*, and often finished off by a year abroad. That training is long and costly, so no doubt it could not be copied in every country. But it is certainly effective, in spite of the obligation it entails to specialise in two different subjects and not one.

The commonest defect, found in many countries, is a lack of correlation between theoretical training, linguistic and cultural, and training in the practice of teaching. The two are often kept quite separate. They are sometimes given in different, even rival, institutions. Another weakness, fortunately less common, is the almost total lack of practical training. That applied to the *Agrégation* in France, which until 1970 required only a one-month practical course, which is a caricature of training for the teaching profession.*

* There is now a one-year training course, but that in-service training leads to no special qualification and is not taken into account in the teacher's career. (D.G.)

To the traditional pattern of training for language teaching, there are some undeniably positive sides. The prospective teacher is given a good general education; and he has a sound general knowledge of the country or countries whose language he is going to teach, especially as a long period abroad has become practically an integral part of his professional training, as has happened as a result of the scheme for the exchange of 'assistants' between Western European countries. He has an excellent knowledge of the foreign literature, which occupies a prominent place in the curriculum and the examinations, and involves a thorough knowledge of the written language and its historical evolution. He will no doubt have studied historical philology in depth. In the course of his studies, written composition in the foreign language and especially translation will have played a very important role and he will have received systematic training in these exercises.

On the other hand, there are some serious gaps. These are revealed as soon as we ask ourselves three crucial questions: *Who* is going to be taught? *What* are we going to teach? *How* are we going to teach it?

The first of these three questions touches on an important range of psychological subjects which are often omitted from the training programme altogether. I refer to all the questions of the theories of learning; of the child's original acquisition of language and the light this may throw on the foreign language learning; of the study of behaviour; the study of motivation and of the individual need for communication; and so forth. A proper initiation into psycho-linguistic problems should be obligatory, instead of being regarded as an optional subject as it now generally is.

To the question "What are we going to teach?" one might give a general answer: a language and the civilisation associated with it. Certainly as far as the language is concerned, historical philology and training in translation would not be sufficient. Modern linguistics, since the days of Ferdinand de Saussure, has turned our attention to synchronic studies and the importance of studying the language of the day. The training of language teachers should include a compulsory initiation into modern linguistics, phonetics and especially phonemics, as well as structural grammar, and lexicology as investigated by quantitive research, with special reference to frequency, usefulness and special vocabularies.

The question "How to teach?" poses the whole question of modern language didactics and that is an extraordinarily complicated one. One can consider it from two different viewpoints. There is first the methodological aspect which involves theoretical, scientific study, and the application to language teaching of linguistic analyses and psychological research. We often speak, in this connection, of 'linguistics applied to language teaching'. It is more a question of applied psycho-linguistics. But there are also a great many practical problems of a purely pedagogical nature, including the application of methodological principles in the classroom, especially through the use of certain techniques, such as audio-visual aids, structural drills, and programmed learning. It is quite clear that traditional training pays all too little attention to such subjects, which have now become of paramount importance.

In sketching brief answers to those three crucial questions, I hope I have thrown into relief the more negative aspects of the basic training which is at present offered in most countries of the world to future language teachers. May we now try to define what might be regarded as the ideal training. It may then be possible to envisage the steps by which we could proceed from the present form of training towards the ideal.

AN IDEAL TRAINING FOR LANGUAGE TEACHERS

Professor Twadell, of Brown University, U.S.A., specified three qualifications which a modern language teacher should have: he must (1) be able to give good models; (2) be a good judge; and (3) be a good master of ceremonies.

To be able to give good models, he must have complete mastery of the language, spoken and written; in other words, a perfect practical knowledge of the language he is teaching.

For him to be a good judge, that practical knowledge is not enough. He must also have a good theoretical knowledge, not only of every aspect of the L2 but also of the characteristics of his pupils' mother tongue, so that he can detect, then correct, and better still prevent, L1 interferences, and take advantage, whenever possible, of points of contact between the two languages, so as to make positive transfers from one to the other. That requires, in particular, a good knowledge of the principles of remedial phonetics. Imitation alone is insufficient. What is needed is *controlled imitation.*

The ability to act as a master of ceremonies is a *sine qua non* of all active teaching. It is no doubt one of the innate talents of a good teacher; but his efficiency will be ten times greater if his classroom techniques have been developed by a special study of what they can accomplish.

The ideal qualifications were summed up at the UNESCO Conference on The Teaching of Modern Languages in Ceylon, in 1953[1], as follows:

1. High standards of attainment in the language (to be taught); correct pronunciation; the ability to read in a clear and expressive manner; fluent and correct speech; facility of expression in writing; and advanced reading ability.

2. Sound linguistic knowledge based on scientific study of the characteristic features of the language, past and present, such as systems of sounds, inflexions, sentence patterns and word formations; and the ability to apply this knowledge in the classroom.

3. Extensive knowledge of the literature and civilisation of the country under study.

4. An introduction to educational psychology and to the theoretical and practical problems of teaching, with special attention to the methods and techniques of teaching foreign languages and the use of audio-visual aids.

It is interesting to note that these four essential points – practical knowledge of the language, linguistic training, acquaintance with the culture, and knowledge of educational psychology – have since been repeated in the recommendations of the Modern Language Association of the U.S.A.[2].

They are also made in the report of the conference organised by B.E.L.C. and the Council of Europe in 1964, referred to earlier, except that the point relating to 'knowledge of the civilisation, etc.' was purposely omitted as it was to be the subject of a separate study[3].

However, the Paris conference provided a framework for the different elements of an ideal form of training, for each category of teachers and in order of priority. The International Federation of Foreign Language Teachers might profitably use this framework for its own recommendations on teacher training.

It is particularly striking that if, at the present time, teacher training appears to be going in different directions in different countries, there is little difficulty in reaching general agreement as to what the ideal goal should be. The problem therefore is to decide by what stages we can one day reach the objectives on which we are generally agreed.

POSSIBLE STEPS TOWARDS A BETTER FORM OF TRAINING

The difficulties we have to overcome are of several kinds. We must first break down the routine, the traditions firmly established, indeed institutionalised, as they have been in France. There is the fact, at which I have already hinted, that the responsibility for training is often shared among institutions which are very jealous of their own prerogatives – for example, universities, teacher training colleges, inspectorates, and centralised administration. There are at times, unfortunately, rivalries between different groups within the teaching profession, each anxious to hold on to its special privileges. Among the difficulties, we must not underestimate the financial implications of any large-scale reform, which is bound to mean the creation of new posts, to raise the question of grants, equipment, and all the rest. That is why it seems reasonable to plan the stages ahead, taking stock of what is immediately feasible and establishing our priorities.

A first stage would consist simply of introducing certain courses into the universities which do not offer them already, by creating chairs of phonetics, general linguistics, applied linguistics, language laboratory technology and psycho-linguistics. Then, students intending to teach foreign languages should be attracted to those new disciplines, and their studies should be recognised by examinations which would at first be optional, then made progressively compulsory. In France, the Association of English Specialists in Higher Education has adopted, and recommended to the Minister of Education, a scheme for re-forming the university degree in English which, while retaining the cultural and literary content of the *licence*, would add perfectly reasonable linguistic requirements to the curriculum.

What would really prove most effective would be the creation of an adequate number of Centres of Applied Linguistics, specialising in linguistic training, and, at the same time, in methodology and the theory and practice of language teaching.

Such centres could be attached to universities, like those that already exist in Britain (e.g. London, Edinburgh, Leeds, Colchester) or in France (Besançon, Nancy, Grenoble). They could be established on the periphery of a university, in the manner of CREDIF and B.E.L.C., which specialise in the teaching of French as a foreign language, or of the Center of Applied Linguistics (CAL) at Washington, the *Centre de Linguistique Appliquée* at Dakar (CLAD), the Centres at Heidelberg and Hamburg in Germany; and others. These Centres are in fact only marginally concerned with the initial training of teachers. Their main activity is concentrated on the further training of teachers already practising, on supplying an information service for them, and on research with the object of developing and trying out methods and teaching materials. However, they could take more part in initial teacher training if they had more substantial funds.

In such ways, the basic training of language teachers could be considerably improved. But until such steps could be taken – progressively, perhaps, as I have suggested – it is important to think out, from now on, the best way of 're-orientating' language teachers who are already at work. That will need in-service training courses which could take various forms.

FURTHER TRAINING

This will have three main objectives:

(a) to fill the gaps in adequate initial training;
(b) to up-date the teacher's proficiency in the language and knowledge of the country, which are always likely to deteriorate with time and contact with his pupils;
(c) to help the teacher keep up with scientific developments in his field which directly concern him, for example in linguistics, psychology and the use of electronic equipment.

In other words, further training will be necessary from the moment that the teacher has finished his basic training, however good the latter may have been. That brings us back to the idea, so dear to Gaston Berger's heart, of 'continuous education', which applies not only to teaching but to every branch of human activity in an age when techniques advance with giant strides. This constant effort to bring oneself up to date, to become 're-orientated', is indispensable for all who have responsibility for imparting knowledge. Teachers could not, without running the risk of doing serious harm, stay happily in a rut and keep out of the march of progress that is going on in every sector of society.

There are usually several ways in which a language teacher can keep himself well-qualified.

He can do so through private reading of books and journals, provided he has time enough and is sure of access to the relevant literature. Information on linguistics and methodology is always available in certain countries at special Information Centres which issue and display book-lists, maintain specialist libraries to which visitors are welcome and do their best to answer your queries. That is done, as far as the teaching of English as a foreign language is concerned, by the Center of Applied Linguistics at Washington, and the English Teaching Information Centre in London. B.E.L.C. endeavours to do the same in Paris for the teaching of French as a foreign language.

The journals specialising in language teaching are particularly useful as instruments of self-training. I have in mind especially the journals of the national associations of language teachers, like *Les Langues Modernes* in France and *Modern Languages* in Britain, which not only serve to keep members of professional bodies informed of their own union affairs, but are increasingly, and quite rightly, assuming the obligation of making the latest developments in linguistics and methodology known to teaching practitioners. On a much wider scale, publications like *English Language Teaching* and *Le Français dans le Monde* have gradually become essential tools of the trade for teachers of English and French, who, in all countries of the world, want to keep in touch with whatever is new in linguistic research and teaching method, as well as with literary and general cultural affairs.

Next, the language teacher can keep himself up to date by enrolling in one of the courses that are now held regularly in certain universities or special centres. They must, of course, have leave of absence for that purpose. In Paris, the Sorbonne has organised seminars for language teachers on the sort of subjects we have been discussing in this book, and in some countries courses along similar lines have been run by correspondence. The tape-recorder has proved extremely useful in providing remedial pronunciation exercises, and the British Institute in Paris has rendered a very welcome service to teachers in the provinces of France who are too far away from university centres, by sending them tape-recordings for that purpose. Radio and television can now replace – or better still, complement – the old form of correspondence course for provincial teachers, for whom the facilities available are thus vastly better than they used to be.

But above all, further training can be given in intensive courses. With the personal contact that these courses provide, they can be very effective so long as they are made to measure and take properly into account:

(a) the level of the teachers concerned;

(b) their actual needs, and the type of teaching they are regularly engaged in;

(c) administrative factors, which have to be thought of well in advance: every detail, including dates, time-tables, financial arrangements, accommodation, equipment, etc., should be taken care of.

Perhaps I could quote from my own experience, having been in charge of an organisation set up to improve methods of teaching French, and therefore responsible for handling around forty courses for teachers of French from different countries and at different levels. On the basis of that experience I would divide in-service training courses into four kinds depending on how much ground one is trying to cover:

(a) **Day courses,** which hardly deserve to be called 'courses' but which can nevertheless serve a useful purpose. These are common in France, and they correspond more or less to the week-end courses which are so popular in Great Britain.

(b) **Short courses,** from ten to fifteen days.

(c) **Medium courses,** from one to three months.

(d) **Long courses,** lasting from six months to a year, or even more. These in fact form part of training in the real sense of the word. They generally complement basic theoretical training and are provided especially

120

for teachers who have had several years of practical teaching experience.

What are the advantages and inconveniences of those four types of course?

The *Day courses* have the advantage that they can be fairly easily arranged for almost every teacher. To be successful, they must, despite the very short time available, have both theoretical and practical content. They should contain some element of linguistic, cultural or methodological information (e.g. by dealing with the theory of audio-visual techniques, for example) and also demonstrate how theory can be put into practice. Teachers like to hear something that they can apply to their daily classroom routine, and they reasonably mistrust abstract dissertations that have no direct bearing on the pedagogical realities that they encounter every day of their lives. Another important thing is to let them have a list of books which are easily obtainable and which they can study at leisure, after receiving in the course an outline of what the books are about. In France, these day courses have developed in the last few years under the aegis of the Ministry of National Education in accordance with recommendations of the Council of Europe. They are usually organised by the regional branches of the Association of Modern Language Teachers with the help of the *Centres Régionaux de Documentation Pédagogiques* (CRDP) and with a grant from the Ministry of Education. In this way, hundreds of language teachers have been able to attend lectures on applied linguistics, with special reference to use of limited vocabularies, the treatment of the spoken language, and structural drills; to see audio-visual methods and techniques in action; and to watch demonstration lessons and then to discuss the effectiveness of the demonstrations afterwards.

Other day courses which are now a regular feature of the educational scene in France are held for future French assistants in Western European countries, or for people who are teaching or going to teach French in North Africa, Equatorial Africa or South-East Asia.

Great Britain organises a great number of week-end courses for similar purposes, and notably in connection with the teaching of foreign languages in the primary school. Denmark, Belgium, Holland and no doubt a number of other countries bring teachers together to study the new audio-visual techniques

and the most effective ways of exploiting the language laboratory. There is no doubt about the usefulness of gatherings of
this kind in making teachers aware of what is new in their
subject. They seem to have good effect, to judge by the very
lively interest shown by the audiences and by such conse-
quences as the demand for book-lists and other complementary
information, the increased subscription for specialised journals,
and the enrolment in longer courses in the same subject. In fact,
the day and week-end courses have done a great deal to arouse
interest in the reform of teaching method. Their effect could be
considerably increased by a larger diffusion of professional
journals, by the establishment of permanent information
centres, and by radio and television broadcasts that would
follow up the story to which these day courses are only an
opening chapter.

The *Short courses* might be regarded as further training
courses in the proper sense. A process of natural selection
operates in them, as they require a greater sacrifice from the
teachers who apply for them − a greater expenditure of time
and energy as well as money. Some of the people who go on
day or week-end courses perhaps do so simply out of curiosity,
mixed with a certain amount of scepticism. For the *short
courses*, a real desire for further training or re-orientation is
essential. So these courses are for people who are really determined and who have problems or interests in common. They
may wish to learn about linguistics, to see how audio-visual
techniques or a language laboratory can help them, how to set
about teaching a foreign language at the primary level, or how
to become qualified in phonetics. The courses may be the
means of determining the careers of future specialists in some
part of the language-teaching field. Practical work can be
properly developed because there is more time. An excellent
example which should be mentioned here is the project of the
Italian Ministry of National Education to put every teacher of
English and French in the technical and classical secondary
schools through staggered ten-day courses. B.E.L.C. was associated with this campaign in respect of the teaching of French
and it takes part annually in five courses organised throughout
the school year in Rome and other big cities in Italy. Similar
courses have been organised in Spain, in France (for teachers of
English), in Israel, Portugal and Tunis, to quote only cases with
which I happen to be personally familiar.

The *Medium courses* are of the same nature as the short ones, except of course that they are more ambitious. With an intensive timetable – generally six hours' classwork a day – and with the heavy load of reading and preparation required, they cover as much ground as a whole year's work in the university. Candidates for these courses are very carefully selected. It is possible to bring teachers to a higher degree of specialisation, and to select those who can be groomed for more important posts in language teaching – such as Advisers and Inspectors.

In the U.S.A., the famous 'NDEA (National Defence Education Act) Institutes', offering eight-week courses, provide an excellent form of re-orientation for secondary school teachers who have an advantage over their colleagues in other countries in that attendance at these courses brings them in a by no means negligible financial benefit. British teachers who are able to attend the three-month course in France have the advantage of receiving real linguistic training, sometimes with spectacular results, thanks to systematic use of the language laboratory. In France, the CREDIF courses turn out experts in the teaching of French by audio-visual methods. A few years ago CREDIF organised a course, for the first time, for the training of trainers and on the strength of it awarded certificates to a strictly selected team of participants. The summer courses held by B.E.L.C. are now performing the same service for various national groups engaged in the teaching of French as L2. Here again, the example of Italy can be quoted: teachers chosen by the Italian authorities to attend this course will be the future language teaching advisers.

The programmes for these courses are drawn up to suit the particular circumstances in the country concerned, and this is ensured by mature teachers who have had sound linguistic training and direct experience of teaching in that particular area. Good examples of this are the medium courses held at Besançon by the French Association of Applied Linguistics or the annual 'Linguistic Institutes' of the American Linguistics Society which are of interest both to linguists and to language teachers.

The *Long courses* offer complementary training, properly speaking. They differ from the basic training courses in that they are not intended for newcomers to the profession but rather for teachers already qualified and experienced, so as to give them a thorough re-training that can often equip them for work of higher responsibility.

In Britain, the Universities of London, Edinburgh, Leeds and some fourteen other universities, are now offering a wide variety of one-year or two-year courses relevant to the teaching of English as a foreign language and to the training of 'English Language Officers' appointed to British Council Centres overseas. On the American side, several universities have a special department for 'TESL' — the Teaching of English as a Second Language — which offer re-training to teachers of American and other nationalities. The English Language Institute of the University of Ann Arbor is the oldest and best known of these centres. The Institute was made famous by the late Professor Fries and his collaborator, Professor Lado, who is now Director of the Institute of Linguistics at Georgetown, where a thorough course specialising in the teaching of English as a foreign language is given. At the University of California at Los Angeles (UCLA), Professor Prator and his colleagues have formed very successful teams of Filipino experts in English teaching who have taken over responsibility for training courses from their American colleagues after working together with them for five years. Those are only some of the examples that could be quoted.

In France, B.E.L.C. has been committed for some years to the organisation of a course to build up a staff of French Language Teaching Advisers for work abroad. There are posts for such Advisers in countries as far apart as Brazil, Cambodia, Ethiopia, Iran, Israel, Mexico, Senegal, Turkey. . . . The basic qualifications required for these posts are as high as one could wish — a good postgraduate degree, Diploma of Education, admission to the Primary Inspectorate; and several years experience of teaching French abroad is compulsory. For this purpose, the object of the further training is to bring the teacher completely up to date in such subjects as linguistics and psycho-linguistics, to familiarise him with the theory and practice of modern methods of language teaching, and with the latest literature in every subject bearing on foreign language teaching, especially French. The syllabus for this course is a very full one, though it concentrates on subjects that were not included in the basic university training. For that reason, there is no literature course; and what generally comes under the heading of 'Civilisation' is only studied inasmuch as it is closely related to the language, and not for its own sake. To give you an idea of the syllabus in detail, I could refer you (and this is not a pure coincidence) to the main headings of the ideal training programme that I have already sketched out. You will find courses in:

(a) **Phonetics**: general phonetics, the phonology of French, comparative phonology;

(b) **General Linguistics**: this course leads to the *Certificat d'Etudes Supérieures* of the Sorbonne;

(c) **Psycho-linguistics**, covering learning theory, and language testing;

(d) **Introduction to teaching by audio-visual aids** (course organised by CREDIF);

(e) **Theoretical and practical courses** at the *Centre International d'Etudes Pédagogiques* at Sèvres, at the Institute of Teachers of French Abroad, and at the Alliance Française.

The members of the course are required, in addition, to present a paper on some problem in linguistics applied to the teaching of French, the subject of the paper − e.g. comparative linguistics, text-book analysis, etc. − depending on the post that the teacher concerned will later be expected to fill. The course we organise at B.E.L.C. is not by any means suggested as a model but only as an example of what it is possible to do in one year's intensive study. The course was originally limited to French teachers, but it is now open to colleagues from other countries provided they have the equivalent of the qualifications required for entry.

We keep in touch with teachers who have been through this course, and this has given us reason to believe that its objects have generally been accomplished: a good teacher has become a real expert and a teacher-trainer capable of organising courses on his own; of compiling models of teaching materials, first in files for internal use, then perhaps for publication; of undertaking original research work on the teaching of French in a given country, involving comparative, psycho- or socio-linguistics; and finally of becoming an adviser who has the ear and the confidence of teachers and educational authorities in the territory to which he is appointed.

Thus, till the day comes − and it is no doubt still distant − when the structure of our universities and administration will have been radically changed and the basic training of language teachers greatly improved, we can at least count on these different types of courses to compensate for some of the deficiencies in existing courses for university degrees.

There will always of course be the unimaginative and unambitious teacher who is quite satisfied with his usual routine, and who will make no effort even to find out what changes have been taking place in his subject once he has finished his university studies. This kind of teacher exists in every subject. I think of the description of a teacher in a book by Jean Onimus entitled *Life and the Teaching of Literature*:[4]

> "You have now been teaching for six years. You know what it is all about, and the system has got you down. Fortunately, you have your tennis and your Sunday outings that can do something to soothe your disillusionment. though the scars will always be there. And your pupils, whom you resemble more and more, will be disillusioned too. You are perfectly content to go on doing what the teachers of the old type of grammar were doing a century ago, except that you will never be as good at it as they were."

Such a teacher is a hopeless case. I prefer the man who does not let the conditions of his job — which I agree are often depressing — defeat him; who is aware of his deficiencies; who is on the look-out for anything that can increase his proficiency; who rushes off to all the week-end courses which his colleague in the category described by Jean Onimus regards with such lordly disdain. This kind of dynamic teacher who is the driving force in his professional association can be very influential. That is the sort of man or woman who makes progress in teaching methods certain.

Still better are those who are prepared to take part in the more important courses which demand not only a more serious interest in further training but also considerable sacrifice in time and money without immediate reward. It is they who will prove to be the best source of recruitment for administrators, inspectors and education advisers — men and women who, one hopes, will owe their appointment not to seniority, not to their docile readiness to toe the right pedagogical line, not even to the fact that they simply happen to have the gift of teaching. It is to be hoped that they will also, and above all, owe their appointment to the fact that they are really well trained, to their interest in keeping themselves abreast of the times and in renewing their knowledge all the time.

At the peak, I would place those teachers who have passed through a sufficiently long course of further training. They would be the people who should be appointed to take charge of the type of re-training I have described above. They could be the inspiration of a centre of applied linguistics like the one in Dakar, that can one day bring about a re-thinking and a re-modelling of language teaching throughout a whole country.

CONCLUSION

I have said that basic training and further training must be complementary. Further training, in so far as it implies the necessity of keeping up to date, is indispensable, however good the basic training may have been. But it is still more useful when the basic training has left out certain essentials altogether, as is often the case. What teachers' associations should do is to fight on two fronts simultaneously, aiming at two objectives:

1. to see that all attempts to reform basic training and to up-date it go ahead, if necessary step by step, so long as progress is made in the right direction;

2. to encourage every form of further training – through specialist journals, permanent courses, information centres, periods of study abroad, seminars at every level – obtaining leave of absence for the purpose and, as far as possible, re-imbursement of the expenses incurred.

It should be recognised once and for all that such activity must be an integral part of the teacher's duties; and I hope that teachers' associations will if necessary make recommendations to that effect.

The authorities of the twenty or so countries who belong to the Council of Europe know that there are official documents which they can refer to in this matter. May I quote one that seems to be entirely unambiguous:

"The Ministers of Education . . . agree to promote the
in-service training of qualified teachers through courses run

in conjunction with teachers' associations, at which courses the teachers will be introduced

> (a) to the results of the work of universities and research institutes in the spoken form of the language and the language used in specialised subjects; and
>
> (b) to new methods of teaching modern languages — for example, the audio-visual methods."[5]

Teachers' associations, especially mentioned in that document, have every right to remind their Ministers, if need be, of those solemn undertakings.

Certainly, we should ask ourselves if we are going on much longer accepting the argument that the best way of learning to teach is to be thrown in at the deep end, so that we sink or swim. Of course, we all know that we can learn a great deal from day-to-day classroom practice. But we also know how expensive, how discouraging and how inconclusive, empirical methods can be. There is no magic in mere teaching experience that can make up for proper linguistic, psychological and methodological training.

Joubert was no doubt right when he said that ";teaching is learning all over again". But we should be wrong to think, as we are inclined to, that by learning his job well in the first place a teacher can be assured that the lessons of experience will then always be profitable. Associations of language teachers in every country must persuade their authorities that there is a better investment still: and that is investment in the training and further training of teachers. For it is on the competence of the teachers, as well as on their enthusiasm, that everything depends.

CONCLUSION

Chapter 8

Towards a Scientific Conception of
Language Teaching

This final chapter is mainly a review of W. F. Mackey's *Language Teaching Analysis*, to which reference has already been made. Mackey's work is very relevant to Girard's general thesis, since it is an outstanding example of the application of linguistic knowledge and methods to the practical problems of foreign language teaching. It is particularly relevant to the very complex tasks of devising a suitable language-teaching methodology and of constructing accurate, well-balanced and effective teaching materials. The author sees Mackey's work as a major step forward towards the establishment of the independent scientific discipline of language didactics envisaged in the introductory chapter of this book.

In his *Language Teaching Analysis*[1] Professor Mackey shows us a clear way towards a scientific conception of our task. The outcome of twenty years of research, it gives pride of place to an objective analysis of 'methods', by which he means language-teaching text-books. His work is undoubtedly the most interesting so far undertaken in a general effort to raise language teaching to the status of an independent discipline by using the procedures of scientific scholarship, with its rigour, its objectivity, its reliance on quantitative evaluation whenever that can be applied, and its rejection of merely personal impressions and hazy approximations.

In order to do this, Mackey began by making a distinction between different areas of investigation. He thus applies his analysis to three major subjects relevant to language teaching, and his work is divided into three parts accordingly:

1. **Language Analysis;**
2. **Method Analysis;** and
3. **Teaching Analysis.**

It is the second of these three parts — the analysis of language text-books — that is by far the most important from our point of view, and it is the most original. Language teachers have every reason to be grateful to Professor Mackey and his team at Laval University for this great work.

In the first part of the book, Mackey passes rapidly over the broad panorama of modern linguistic studies, dividing the field into four parts: *Language Theory* ("Language-teaching methods and the teaching of them", he tells us, "depend ultimately on what the teacher or method-maker thinks a language is"[2]), *Language Description, Language Differences*, and *Language Learning*. As we saw in an earlier chapter, the scene is not very encouraging for the novice who seeks the truth about language and who will be dismayed to discover that, as in other areas of human experience, truth is by no means undivided. Remember, anyone who wishes to practise 'applied linguistics' is bound to be faced with the problem of what kind of linguistics to apply.

There are a few gaps in Professor Mackey's overall picture of the modern linguistic world. The reader might regret the brevity with which — in one paragraph — *Language Teaching Analysis* disposes of transformational-generative theories. Whatever one's opinion of them, those theories constitute a radical and very significant contribution to modern linguistics. Unfortunately, the book leaves them largely unexplained. You will find no mention of them in the otherwise very full index, either under 'transformational' or 'generative' grammar.

However, as they stand, Mackey's two introductory chapters on linguistic theories and descriptions are a very useful digest of different models of language analysis; though this does not exempt us from more detailed reading on the subject. They are followed by a chapter on language differences which provides a good illustration of the value of comparative studies; and then by a chapter on psycho-linguistics, dealing with the acquisition of the mother-tongue and subsequently of other languages.

Then we come to the heart of the book, Part Two, in which Professor Mackey devotes nearly two hundred pages to the application of his techniques to a scientific analysis of language teaching text-books. With the aid of computers, he has produced a highly detailed quantitative analysis of the contents of the text-books examined. Just as the study of machine translation, through the rigour that mechanical treatment exacts, has speeded up progress in linguistic research, so by similar methods Professor Mackey's research has unquestionably increased our knowledge and control of the methodology of language teaching. We need no longer be satisfied with a subjective assessment of a text-book as we aimlessly turn over its pages to form a personal judgement on the arrangement, the quality of the illustrations, the likely appeal of the texts or the soundness of such-and-such an exercise that happens to have caught our eye. What Professor Mackey has attempted has been akin to the acoustic analysis that can be made of a stream of speech in a phonetics laboratory: he has picked out a number of *parameters* – factors which must be present in one form or another in every method but which vary in detail from case to case – and he has subjected each one to painstaking investigation.

The parameters he deals with can be divided into four main sectors:

1. the *selection* of the linguistic items taught in a course;

2. the *gradation* by which these items are presented;

3. the *presentation* of these items in a way intended to ensure comprehension; and

4. the *repetition* of the items through a range of oral and written exercises designed to help the pupils remember the material taught and to convert it into their own active knowledge.

Those four divisions correspond exactly with the four main stages, defined by Halliday, McIntosh and Strevens[3], by which they maintain a text-book should be systematically compiled. Halliday and his colleagues only give us the outlines of those four stages: Mackey examines the entire process in the most precise detail.

The *selection* of items will first of all be modified by three variables, which are: the *purpose* of the course and therefore of the selection; the *level* of the pupils for whom the course is intended; and its *duration* and the timetable at one's disposal.

Before selecting the linguistic items he proposes to include in his course, the text-book writer must make three preliminary decisions: he must decide on the *type* of language to be taught – which dialect, register and style, whether spoken or written; on the *number* of items in each category, including nouns, verbs, adjectives, adverbs, structure words, etc.; on the very important question of *choice of criteria* to be adopted, and on their order of priority. With regard to the last point, it will soon be evident that there is often a conflict between the different criteria one chooses. Professor Mackey adopts five criteria, namely:

1. *frequency* – how often an item is used in real communication;
2. *range* – how widely it is used, i.e. in how many different types of the language;
3. *availability* – how indispensable it is in certain situations;
4. *coverage* – how many other items it could displace; and
5. *learnability* – how easily it can be learnt.

It is not until he has taken his decisions on these points that the text-book writer can justifiably decide which phonological and grammatical items, which items of vocabulary and which different meanings, to include in his course.

When he comes to making quantitative measurements within the sector of selection, Mackey concentrates on seven quantifiable parameters. These are:

1. the *amount* of material included in the course;

    the *proportion* of
2. nouns,
3. verbs,
4. adjectives,
5. adverbs;

6. *frequency*; and
7. *range*

To measure 1, the amount, he determines the percentage of different words found in the course in relation to the total number of words in a well-known frequency list, such as the *General Service Word List* compiled by Michael West. He then calculates the proportion of nouns, verbs, adjectives and adverbs. That leaves parameters 6 (frequency) and 7 (range), which he measures by expressing the total of the indices in terms of percentages of the grand total number of words occurring in the corpus from which the frequency list was originally taken. The figures obtained for each parameter have no virtue in themselves; but as soon as you begin to compare the results for two different methods — provided, of course, the same standards of measurements were used in both cases — you have plenty of data for sound conclusions on the question of how systematically the course was planned, at least in respect of its lexical content.

To measure *gradation*, Mackey chooses eleven further parameters, namely: (1) *productivity* ('How much can you say with what you have?'); and ten aspects of *intake* ('How much comes in at a time?'). The ten aspects of intake are: (2) nouns, (3) verbs, (4) adjectives, (5) adverbs, (6) structure words, (7) inflections, (8) sentence structures, (9) clause structures, (10) phrase structures and (11) formulas, or idiomatic expressions. To measure these, he uses as a general formula a very simple device which starts by dividing the total number of words in the course by the number of words that are different. Thus, if the first number is 16,750 and the second 596, the result is 28, which means that each word occurs in the course twenty-eight times on an average. One then has to examine the distribution of the twenty-eight occurrences. This simple formula increases in importance as it is progressively applied to the ten aspects of intake specified above.

Presentation is measured by taking two groups of four parameters each. The first group is concerned with the four modes of *expression* — listening, speaking, reading, writing; and in this group calculations are made to answer the question 'How much of one skill is introduced before how much of another?' The second group is concerned with *content*; and in this group measurements are taken of the *differential* — the percentages of L1 and L2 words in relation to the total number of running words in the course; of the *ostensive* element, answering the question 'How much of the presentation of meaning must the teacher do through objects, actions and situations?'; of the *pictorial* element essential to the explanation of meaning; and of the *contextual*, i.e. presentation through contexts.

The fourth main sector, *repetition*, is the one most searchingly investigated, since it is divided into eighteen parameters covering (1) the *number* of exercises; the *distribution* of exercises according to (2) vocabulary, and (3) structure; the *ratio* of (4) listening exercises, (5) speaking exercises (6) reading,' and (7) writing, to the grand total; the *media* or nature of the supporting material, i.e. (8) texts, (9) recordings and (10) pictures; the *variety* of exercises, again according to the four basic skills of (11) listening, (12) speaking, (13) reading, and (14) writing; and the basic *types* of exercise, i.e. (15) rote or simple repetition, (16) incremental, i.e. expression by means of expansion, etc., (17) variational or modification, and (18) operational, by transfer or other means.

That accounts for a total of forty-four parameters investigated in a very impressive operation, which could not have been performed without the assistance of computers. However, that total is not exhaustive, and, as Professor Mackey admits, it is insufficient for a complete study of the problem. It is rather surprising, in fact, that the first main sector, selection, is the least favoured in the analysis, in so far as only seven parameters in it are considered. One might have expected to find in it all the parameters included in the gradation sector: and the question arises: why pick out nouns, verbs, adjectives and adverbs for special attention, while grammatical structure and usage are not treated at all? Moreover, one might wonder why the two criteria of frequency and range have been chosen for special treatment, while the three others — availability, coverage and learnability — have been left out of the calculations. The author himself answers these objections by deploring the lack of background statistical studies which would have provided standards of measurement comparable with those which word frequency counts have made available to us. A mathematical study of grading is relatively straightforward because it can be carried out within the limits of each course, and percentages can simply be expressed in relation to the corpus of material included in that particular text-book. On the other hand, in the selection sector, comparisons have to be made either with a much wider corpus or with the language as a whole. It is a fact that, in the area of selection, the only aspect of a language that has been the subject of statistical investigations is the lexicon; and even that aspect has only been studied in respect of frequency, range, and — in the case of French — availability. However, since the publication of *Language Teaching Analysis*, Professor Mackey, in collaboration with J. G. Savard, has made a special study of coverage in the lexicon of French[4]. He has drawn up a list of 3,000 words in decreasing order of coverage value, and has thus provided writers of French language-textbooks with a useful selection criterion which will help us to complete and correct the Basic French Word-list (*le français fondamental*). Having done that work on coverage in French, Professor Mackey is now in a position to add an eighth parameter to his selection sector, at least as far as French text-books are concerned.

There is another parameter that is unfortunately missing from both the first and the second sectors, namely *comparison with the mother-tongue.* This seems to me so important in a foreign language text-book that I would certainly add it to the criteria that affect the choice of material to be included. Professor Mackey could well reply that we do not have an adequate standard of measurement for it at hand. Then again, could it not be argued that the notion of the *productivity* of linguistic items, which heads the list of the eleven parameters of gradation, is also a useful criterion in selection? I think it could be, although I realise that there too we have no real statistical data for any language. Meanwhile, the criteria of comparison with the mother-tongue and of productivity are matters that the text-book writer must decide empirically, until such time as he can base his decisions on precise information supplied by objective analysis.

The reader will probably be wondering what is produced when Professor Mackey has sifted and analysed a collection of teaching material in this meticulous manner. The immediate answer to that question must be the negative one that Professor Mackey does not pretend to reach any conclusion at all, in that he is not concerned with *judging* a course, only with *analysing* it. So he does not tell us that Course A is better than Course B. He only points out that they are different and shows us at what points they diverge. He shows us the differences very clearly by means of what he calls a *'Method Profile'.* Each profile looks like an irregular star with eight or ten long points, in the middle of a circular spider's web. The circle is divided into forty-four equal sections, corresponding to his forty-four parameters. The 'star' is in fact a graph formed by lines joining up the points which mark the different percentages obtained for each parameter, 0 per cent being at the centre of the circle and 100 per cent at the circumference.

Judgement, in the form of a comparison between one method and another from the point of view of their effectiveness, will come later, when the analysis of each text-book has been complemented by an analysis of the results obtained through the use of that text-book. We are perhaps better prepared for that complementary kind of analysis, now that we have batteries of tests for testing control of linguistic material taught. By means of such tests, System Development Corporation of Los Angeles, under the direction of M. G. Newmark, has published a comparative study of the results obtained through the use of three text-books for teaching Spanish to English-speaking beginners at the primary school level[5]. Comparing Mackey's 'Method Profile' with the results of control tests, it might one day be possible to say what is the ideal 'method profile' for a given situation; in other words, to say what profile is likely to produce the best results, other things being equal. In that way, teachers would have a precise instrument for evaluating a text-book; and text-book writers would be encouraged to draw up their courses, stage by stage, more systematically. We could in that way produce norms which text-book writers and teachers would do well to respect. Is that a utopian view of how a text-book ought to be compiled? I do not think it is, although we should not hide the fact that we still have a long way to go before we reach that stage. There is bound to be resistance to what might be regarded as a scientific tyranny in these matters. Nevertheless, within the limitations of the norms produced in the way I envisage, there would still be a considerable margin of freedom for the individual author. What I think we must do is find a happy medium between excessive control and the unbelievable anarchy that we have today. As an example of that anarchy, in the vocabularies of the three text-books tested by M. G. Newmark and quoted above, there are only fifty content words in common!

The third part of Mackey's work is devoted to an analysis of teaching procedures practised in the classroom. A text-book can serve no purpose by itself: it must be suitable for the syllabus, for the pupil and for the teacher. In the first chapter of the third part of the book, the author therefore discusses *the suitability of methods*, and the use the teacher will actually make of the text-book he has. The author then goes on to discuss how far the teacher is free or is likely to depart from the text-book in the *language* he actually teaches his pupils; how far the planning of actual lessons should or does follow the *plan* followed by the text-book writer; and the various classroom *techniques* by which individual teachers can present and drill their material according to particular circumstances.

Then follow a chapter on *automated language teaching*, with special reference to language laboratories, and one on *measurement of language learning* by means of tests of various kinds. In the first of these two chapters it is a pity that no proper mention is made of teaching machines and programmed learning. There is, it is true, a passing allusion to teaching machines in a paragraph on visual aids, but then only from a technical viewpoint and with no reference to the basic theory of programming. In fact, one could make a general criticism of the chapter on automation on the grounds that it concentrates on the technical aspect, on the 'hardware', enumerating the different types of language laboratories, rather than on their methodological side and on the 'software'. It is also unfortunate that while visual aids and auditory aids are dealt with, they are only treated separately; integrated audio-visual teaching, with its firm theoretical basis, is omitted altogether.

The final chapter, on the measurement of learning, is a parallel to the last chapter of Part Two, which is on the measurement of method. It is rather disappointing that the final chapter did not deal, instead, with the measurement of *teaching* or of *linguistic pedagogy*. It is understandable that parameters for the analysis of language teaching would be more difficult to determine than for method analysis; and we know that Professor Mackey has done some interesting research on the effectiveness of language teaching[6]. He has, for example, used various devices to facilitate the analysis and measurement of the teacher's speaking time compared with the pupils', of the time spent on each phase of the language lesson, and so on. However, by giving his book the title *Language Teaching Analysis* did he not have in mind the ultimate measurement of language teaching?

Such criticisms do not, need I say, detract from the importance of Mackey's book, with which every language teacher ought to be thoroughly familiar. To make it still more important, the work ends with a bibliography of more than ninety pages, listing no fewer than 1,741 titles of books and articles, classified in an order corresponding to that of the chapters of the book itself. In subjects as active as linguistics and language methodology, it is difficult to produce exhaustive bibliographies and impossible to keep them up to date. There are in consequence certain omissions, despite the length of the bibliography, that might seem surprising. However, that is hardly the author's fault. The book took several years to pass through the process of publication. It was submitted to the publisher in

1961, and the few books that appeared after that date and have been included in the bibliography were added at the proof stage. The bibliography is none the less an invaluable source of information for anyone concerned with language teaching.

To conclude this chapter, I should perhaps justify the title chosen for it. If language teaching has made notable progress in the last quarter of a century, that is not due, as insistent publicity would have us believe, to the magical properties of machinery. I would be the first, as a pioneer in their use, to acknowledge the services that can be rendered by tape-recorders, projectors, language laboratories, even teaching machines, provided they are used wisely. But, as I have said before, they are *technical devices* in the service of a *methodology*, and it is the methodology that is primarily responsible for the results, good or bad, of the new teaching. The great difference between modern and traditional methods is to be found in the rigorous scientific attitude with which we now approach the target language and the psychological problems of language learning. Today, neither the text-book writer nor the language teacher can be allowed to rely solely on his own instincts. The *content* of the text-book, of the course and of each lesson in it, should be in accordance with a sound linguistic analysis of the language taught and of the differences between that language and the students' mother tongue. The same applies to *grading*: the language cannot be taught all at once, but by a succession of steps which can only be reliably determined by linguistic research, in accordance with scientific criteria and statistical studies. When we come to *presenting* the linguistic material we have selected and graded, whether for the text-book or for the classroom, then we must depend on psychology, and scientifically-conducted experiments in that field, for guidance on such questions as whether comprehension and memorisation are best achieved through pictures or auditory media; how positive is the contribution of tape-recorders and language laboratories; what are the most effective pedagogical techniques in normal classroom conditions. Similarly, the different types of *exercises* and *tests* that we use should now be decided scientifically and should not be a matter of purely personal judgement.

So has language teaching at last become an exact science? We are a long way off from that yet. There is still a great deal of research to be done. And the fact remains that teaching will always be a human activity that can never be entirely mechanised. Those who are scared by the progress of science and technology, who regard it as dehumanising and as slavery to machines, can rest assured. In so far as a more effective methodology will ease and shorten the process of language learning, far from enslaving the learner, it will set him free more quickly, by giving him a speedier means of enriching and developing his cultural store.

In the movement 'towards a scientific conception of language teaching', Mackey's masterly work is an important milestone. By subjecting language teaching methods to such meticulous scrutiny, evaluating them precisely with the support of figures rather than through vague impressions, he has not only made it easier for us to assess them but he has given us a set of criteria for compiling better text-books in future. He has done text-book writers a great service. As for the teacher, the text-book user, he should keep Professor Mackey's book by him for constant reference. It will surely help him to see the fundamental problems of his profession in a new light, and will lead him towards the yet unseen horizons of the language teaching of tomorrow.

APPENDIX

Different Types of Structural Drills

(Translation of an article, by Geneviève Delattre, of the University of California, Santa Barbara, which appeared in *Le Français dans le Monde*, No. 41, June 1966.) A few comments by the translator have been added, in square brackets; and some of the items have been omitted from the examples, in view of the length of the article.

To pretend to give an exhaustive list of all the possible types of structural drills would be presumptuous. Such drills can assume a wide variety of forms since their purpose is to provide a systematic and strictly controlled manipulation of the many constituent parts of a language. Any classification of them is bound to be arbitrary. According to whether one reckons only the main categories, or includes all the possible combinations of one type with another, figures for the total number of basic types differ considerably. Nelson Brooks[1], for example, gives twelve types; Robert Lado[2] fourteen; and Robert Politzer[3] seven. Nomenclature, also, often varies, the same types of drill being named differently by different authors. I therefore trust the reader will forgive a certain arbitrariness on my own part, as regards both the classification adopted in this essay and the name given to each type of drill.

My division into *seven categories* is determined by the basic mechanisms by which the structural drills operate. Certain of these categories — substitution and controlled dialogues, in particular — include types of drill which are sufficiently different from one another to merit separate examination and therefore to constitute secondary categories on their own. So as to present as clear and as helpful a picture as possible to those readers who may not yet be very familiar with structural drills, I shall try to describe each type with the minimum of technical terminology. I shall examine the form of each drill — that is to say, how it is constructed and developed — and its aim. Each description will be followed by an example and by a few linguistic or pedagogical comments. Although the examples I have chosen are almost entirely intended for the teaching of grammatical structure, it does not necessarily follow that the types of drill described are applicable to grammar only: they can serve other purposes as well.

REPETITION

This is the simplest kind of exercise — so simple, in fact, that one hesitates to call it a structural drill at all. However, it is fundamental and is the starting point for most of the other drills.

Form. The teacher asks the pupils to listen to, then to repeat after him, a series of sentences containing the structural opposition[4] that is to be taught. In pronouncing each sentence, the teacher and pupils alike should follow the natural intonation contour. The teacher should not try to stress the elements that are in opposition to each other, and the pupils should not be allowed to distort the suprasegmental features of the foreign language — that is to say, the intonation, rhythm, stress or way an utterance is divided into syllables.

Example [FROM FRENCH]. Presentation of the definite article. The drill consists of three or more model sentences for each of the five forms of the definite article: masculine singular before a consonant /lə/, feminine singular before a consonant /la/, masculine and feminine singular before a vowel /l/, masculine and feminine plural before a consonant /le/, and masculine and feminine plural before a vowel /lez/. Thus:

Le professeur est ici.	(The teacher is here)
Le livre est ici.	book
Le crayon est ici.	pencil
Voilà la gare.	(There is the station.)
Voilà la bibliothèque.	library.
Voilà la table.	table.
Tu cherches l'église?	(You're looking for the church?)
Tu cherches l'hôtel?	hotel?
Tu cherches l'école?	school?

Où sont les cahiers?	(Where are the exercise books?)
Où sont les chaises?	chairs?
Où sont les cinémas?	cinemas?

Voilà les étudiantes.	(There are the students.)
Voilà les enfants.	children.
Voilà les autos.	cars.

Example [FROM ENGLISH]. As the definite article in English has only two forms in fluent speech — /ð ə/ before a consonant sound and /ði/ before a vowel sound — its phonological form would require a much simpler drill than the definite article in French. Thus:

1. There's the door.
   There's the light.
   There are the stairs.

2. Where's the ink?
   Where are the apples?
   Where are the oranges?

However, readers should have no difficulty in thinking of other aspects of English grammatical structure that would lend themselves to presentation in this way.

Aim. This drill replaces the grammatical explanation that used to be given by traditional methods. In this case, the grammatical point is presented in a linguistic context. The pupils are obliged to perceive *aurally* the opposition illustrated by the model sentences. They must then reproduce that opposition in the form in which it came to them in a context; and they should be able to understand, through comparison and analogy, how the opposition functions. The repetition of the sentences by the pupils makes it possible for them to develop auditory habits and articulatory habits at the same time. Moreover, recent psychological experiments seem to suggest that the mere fact of articulation aids comprehension and reinforces capacity to memorise the models.

Comment. By its very simplicity, repetition as a drill has its limitations and dangers. It should only be used for the initial presentation of a new linguistic item, and the teacher should be careful not to let it go on to the point of boredom. When that point is reached, nothing further is achieved by repeating the models. Furthermore, it is essential that the repetition drill should be conducted by the teacher at a fairly rapid pace, and in such a way that each sentence keeps its natural melody. One more point: if the item being taught can be presented in different sentence-types, as in the example above, the repetition drill will also serve as practice in typical rhythms and intonation patterns.

It must be made quite clear to the pupils from the start that the object of such an exercise is not to pump the foreign language into them, but that mental activity is just as necessary in this kind of drill as aural perception and oral reproduction. The repetition drill should be so constructed as to present a clear solution to a grammatical problem. *Drawing the pupils' attention to what they are hearing and repeating, and making them discover for themselves what new morphological or syntactical feature they are learning, is an essential part of the repetition drill.* It is perhaps not a waste of time to insist on this point so that misunderstanding can be cleared up once and for all. None of the drills that we are going to consider can be really effective if the pupils are not trained, from the beginning, to understand what they are doing. Just as it is natural to grasp the precise reference of a word or phrase without formulating a semantic rule for it, so it is possible, and desirable, to understand the grammatical significance of a structural opposition or contrast without formulating a *grammatical* rule.

SUBSTITUTION

So that we can understand the mechanism of substitution exercises, which have many forms, let us consider a sentence as being composed of a certain number of segments, each one within a frame, the position of which is in a fixed relation to the position of other frames. Each frame can hold a certain class of segments only. By substituting one segment for another within the same frame, we retain the general structure of the sentence but change its semantic content. However, because in every language there is a certain amount of inherent redundancy[5], it often happens that a substitution introduced into one frame necessitates a modification of one or more segments in other frames. For example:

146

Le	*livre*	*est*	*sur*	*la*	*table*
1	2	3	4	5	6
The	book	is	on	the	table

Suppose, in French, we replace *Le* in frame 1 by *Les*. We must then replace *est* in frame 3 by *sont*. I am only considering the oral realisation of the sentence. In writing, we should also have to replace *livre* by *livres*, but this would not affect the oral structure of the sentence. [On the other hand, in English the sentence would now be *The books are on the table*, a substitution occurring in frame 2, and *is* being changed to *are* in frame 3.] A substitution drill can be *simple* or more or less *complex*, according to whether a substitution in one frame necessitates changes in the other frames. We shall consider four types of substitution drill.

1
SIMPLE SUBSTITUTION

Form. Here, substitution takes place only in one frame, and in the same frame throughout the drill. It must not require modification in any of the other frames. In other words, the sentence is changed on the semantic level exclusively. The teacher presents the basic structure that he wants the pupils to practise. He demonstrates, by giving a model, in what way and in what frame the substitution is to operate. He begins the drill with the pupils, giving them the basic sentence, then the alternative segment which is to be fitted in. The pupils – in chorus, then individually – carry out the substitution. The teacher then supplies the next alternative segment, and so on. Here are two examples:

Example (1) Drill for *habiter à* (= live in) in contrast with its English counterpart, starting from the basic sentence *J'habite à Paris* (I live in Paris):

PUPILS		TEACHER
J'habite à (I live in)	*Paris.*	*(Rome)*
	Rome.	*(Chicago)*
	Chicago.	*(Santa Barbara)*
	Santa Barbara.	and so on.

Example (2) Drill for verbs (in French) which take an indirect object followed by *de* (= to) plus an infinitive, starting from the basic sentence *Il dit à son ami de venir* (He tells his friend to come):

PUPILS		TEACHER
Il dit à son ami de venir.		*(demande)* (= asks)
demande	*à son ami de venir.*	*(propose)* (=proposes)
propose	*à son ami de venir.*	*(conseille)* (= advises)
conseille		*(répond)* (= replies)
répond		*(ordonne)* (= orders)
ordonne		and so on.

[Readers will see at once that the basic sentence structure in this particular case will be different in French and English. In 'He tells his friend to come' there is no preposition equivalent to the French *à*. Moreover, *asks, advises* and *orders* can be substituted for *tells* in the English sentence, but *proposes* and *replies* will require a different sentence structure. Furthermore, *wants, expects* and other English verbs could replace *tells*, whereas their French equivalents could not replace *dit* in the basic structure. Here is a case, therefore, where different drills would have to be constructed for English and for French, and where a comparison of the differences could be revealing.]

Aim. Whereas the repetition drill initiates the pupil into a certain structure, the simple substitution drill enables him to begin to assimilate that structure. . . . The variation within a single frame teaches him to recognise and use the class of segment which can fit into that frame, while preventing him from distorting the structure. He thus learns to recognise the possibilities of the structure, as well as its limitations. On the other hand, he learns to recognise the limitations of each constituent segment, since — as we have seen — only certain items can be used in the process of substitution.

Comment. Although substitution drills can be used for the teaching of vocabulary (for example, when the teacher shows a picture illustrating a new word which can at once be fitted into the appropriate frame), they are mostly used to give practice in a certain structure. For that reason, it is best to use only lexical items that are already known, so that the pupil's attention is concentrated on the grammatical mechanism and not on the meaning of new vocabulary. As simple substitution drill is easy, it should be conducted at a fairly fast pace and only a short time should be spent on it. It could soon become monotonous, and the pupils' attention would then wander: this could be prevented for a time if the teacher, by a system of signs which the class understood, called for responses now from the class as a whole, now from individual members of it. Like the repetition drill, the simple substitution drill is generally speaking a preparation for a more difficult exercise in which the pupil must either make a correct choice or immediately find the right correlation between two or more segments in the sentence.

2

MULTIPLE PROGRESSION

Form. Here, instead of making the substitution in only one frame, the pupil must make it alternately in two or three frames, without effecting any changes in the grammatical structure. For each new segment that the teacher gives them, they must immediately decide to which frame it belongs: that means they must identify the grammatical nature of the new segment, deciding in effect whether it is a noun, verb, adjective or adverb.

Example (1) From the simple substitution drill described above, we can move on to the *bipartite progression drill* such as the following, in which the English-speaking student practises the use of *à* + the name of a city or town, where in English one would have to choose between *in* and *to* according to whether the verb indicates movement or otherwise. Thus:

PUPILS	TEACHER
J'habite à (I live in) *Paris*	*(Chicago)*
J'habite à Chicago.	*(Je vais)*
Je vais à (I'm going to) *Chicago.*	*(Londres)*
Je vais à Londres.	*(Je rentre)*
Je rentre à (I'm going back to) *Londres.*	*(Bordeaux)*
Je rentre à Bordeaux.	*(J'arrive)*
J'arrive à (I'm arriving in) *Bordeaux.*	*(Rome)*
J'arrive à Rome.	*(Je suis)*
Je suis à (I'm in) *Rome.*	*(Paris)*
Je suis à Paris.	and so on.

F

[Again, a different drill would have to be constructed for English, so as to practise the opposition between *I live in . . .* and *I'm going to . . .*]

Example (2) *Tripartite progression*

PUPILS	TEACHER
Elle cherche un quartier tranquille. (She is looking for a quiet district)	*(élégant)* (= smart)
Elle cherche un quartier élégant.	*(chapeau)* (= hat)
Elle cherche un chapeau élégant.	*(prend)* (= is taking)
Elle prend un chapeau élégant.	*(rouge)* (= red)
Elle prend un chapeau rouge.	*(livre)* (= book)
Elle prend un livre rouge.	*(achète)* (= is buying)
Elle achète un livre rouge.	*(intéressant)* (= interesting)
Elle achète un livre intéressant.	*(cherche)*
Elle cherche un livre intéressant.	*(quartier)*
	– and so on.

Aim. The pupils must choose the frame in which the substitution will operate in each case, and in this way they learn to distinguish between the different word-classes. The drill thus makes them explore the possibilities of semantic variation within a given structural framework. It goes without saying that the meaning of the words chosen by the teacher must be known to the class before the drill begins. Multiple progression drills can therefore provide practice in assimilating both grammatical structures and newly-acquired vocabulary.

Comment. This kind of drill must be constructed very carefully since each new segment given by the teacher must fit perfectly and without ambiguity into one single frame. Thus in the last example, if that drill were done in English, the teacher would have to take care to present *looking for* as one lexical item fitting into the same frame as *taking* and *buying*. As the model sentence is being changed all the time, the pupils usually find it difficult to decide what the last link in the chain should be. The drill will therefore proceed more smoothly if, after each substitution, the teacher repeats the changed sentence so that the pupils know exactly in what sentence they have to make the next substitution. Thus:

TEACHER (repeating): *Elle prend un livre rouge. (achète)*
PUPILS: *Elle achète un livre rouge.*
TEACHER: *Elle achète un livre rouge.*
(intéressant)
PUPILS: *Elle achète un livre intéressant.*
and so on.

3
SUBSTITUTION BY EXPANSION OR REDUCTION

Form. Instead of keeping to a fixed number of frames in the model sentence, with each new segment filling one single frame, we can make substitutions which result in increasing the number of frames or decreasing them. In other words, the basic sentence is lengthened or shortened.

An example of expansion:

FRENCH	ENGLISH
Il est arrivé hier (hier soir)	He arrived yesterday (yesterday evening)
Il est arrivé hier soir. (Le garçon)	He arrived yesterday evening. (The boy)
Le garçon est arrivé hier soir. (Le jeune garçon)	The boy arrived yesterday evening. (The young boy)
Le jeune garçon est arrivé hier soir (hier soir à neuf heures)	The young boy arrived yesterday evening (yesterday evening at nine o'clock)
Le jeune garçon est arrivé hier soir à neuf heures.	The young boy arrived yesterday evening at nine o'clock.

Substitution by reduction would work the other way round, starting from a long sentence from which appropriate segments would be progressively removed.

Aim. In addition to semantic variations such as are produced in the preceding drills, we now have progressive structural sophistication, and the experience of proceeding from the simple to the complex, as well as of exploring the possibilities of expanding and reducing the sentence. Like the previous drills, this is one more stage in the acquisition of the basic mechanisms of the second language.

Comment. The above drill can be carried out in several phases. So as to grade the difficulties, one might begin by limiting the expansion to the noun phrase (or nominal group) functioning as the subject of the sentence. Then one could start the exercise again, concentrating this time on expanding the adverbial phrase. Those two steps would amount to no more than a modification of the simple substitution drill. In a third step, one could proceed to progressive substitution in both the noun phrase and the adverbial phrase, taking care to give the whole phrase that is to be included and not merely the fragment that is to be added. There can be a fourth and final step which we shall come to later, under EXPANSION.

4
CORRELATION

Form. This is a substitution drill in which the new segment requires one or more changes in other frames. It proceeds in the same way as the other substitution drills.

Example (1) Correlation of the segment in frame 2 with the segment in frame 1. Drill on the Present Tense of the verb *avoir* (= have).

1 2   3

Jean a   une soeur. (Paul et Henri)

Paul et Henri ont	*(Tu)*
Tu as	*(Vous)*
Vous avez	*(Je)*
J'ai	*(Nous)*
Nous avons	*(Elle)*
Elle a	*(Elles)*
Elles ont	and so on

1   2 3

John has a sister.

Paul and Henry	have
You (singular)	have
You (plural)	have
I	have
We	have
She	has
They (feminine)	have

152

Example (2) Correlation of the segments in frames 2 and 3 with the segment in frame 1. Drill on the possessive adjectives.

1 2 3	1 2 3
J'aime bien mon cours de français. (nous)	I like my French course very much.
Nous aimons bien notre cours de français. (Jacques)	We our
Jacques aime bien son cours de français. (Jacques et Claudine)	Jack likes his . . .
Jacques et Claudine aiment bien leur cours de français. (Tu)	Jack and Claudine like their etc.
Tu aimes bien ton cours de français. (Il)	You like your . . .
Il aime bien son cours de français. (Ils)	He likes his . . .
Ils aiment bien leur cours de français. (Elle)	They like their . . .
Elle aime bien son cours de français.	She likes her . . .
and so on.	

Aim. This kind of drill is perhaps the most widely used in audio-lingual teaching, as it can help the pupil to learn to manipulate the whole morphology of the language without separating it from syntax and without isolating one form from another. It replaces the paradigms by which conjugations, pronouns, etc. used to be taught.

Comment. Theoretically, we could have correlation of the segment in frame 2 with that in frame 1, i.e. requiring the pupil to select the 'right answer' for frame 2; or we could have it the other way round, i.e. requiring the pupil to select the right answer for frame 1. In practice, the former procedure is almost always adopted, the teacher giving a new item for frame 1 every time. Substitution drills, to be effective both in the classroom and in the language laboratory, require only one correct answer — without any possible alternative — at each step in the transformation of the basic sentence. If the teacher changes a word in frame 2 and then expects the pupil to provide the 'right answer' for frame 1, he will constantly find that a number of alternative answers are possible. For example, in English, *have* in position 2 could produce *I* or *we* or *you* or *they* in position 1, just as, in French, *ont* in position 2 could produce *ils* or *elles* in position 1. As sentences in both French and English follow a strict word order, and as we are not in the habit of speaking backwards, it is hardly likely that the teacher *would* expect the pupils to work from position 2 to position 1, except of course in the interrogative (e.g. *A quelle heure partez-vous?* -- At what time do you leave?) and in the imperative of French reflexive verbs (e.g. *Levez-vous* -- Stand up).

Variations

(1) Instead of triggering off changes in one or more other frames in the sentence, the alternative segment given by the teacher might itself have to undergo a change when it takes its place in the context. For example, the teacher could give the infinitive of a verb, leaving the pupils to put the verb into its right form, or he could give the singular form of a noun and the pupils would have to supply the plural.

Examples

(a) *Crois-tu qu'il vienne demain?*   Do you think he'll
    (écrire)   come tomorrow?
  Crois-tu qu'il écrive demain?   write
    (partir)
  Crois-tu qu'il parte demain?   leave
  and so on.

[There would be no point in doing a drill in that particular form in English; but there would be in example (b)]

(b) *Je n'aime pas les animaux.*   I don't like animals. (horse)
    (cheval)
  Je n'aime pas les chevaux.   horses. (mouse)
    (souris)
  Je n'aime pas les souris.   mice.   (egg)
    (oeuf)
  Je n'aime pas les oeufs. etc.   eggs.

(2) Combining correlation with simple substitution or with multiple progression, one can get a more varied kind of drill with many more semantic variations.

Example: Drill for adjectives, in the plural, before or after a noun. [This drill, too, would be very useful in French, though in English there would be less in it for the pupil to do.]

Nous avons lu de beaux livres.	*(vu)*
vu	*(films)*
films.	*(bons)*
bons	*(Je)*
J'ai	*(intéressants)*
des films intéressants.	*(amis)*
amis	

We've read some fine books.	(seen)
seen	(films)
films.	(good)
good	(I)
I've	(interesting)
interesting films.	(friends)
friends.	

TRANSFORMATION

Form. Now, instead of transforming a model sentence step by step, replacing one segment at a time by another, the pupils hear a series of sentences given by the teacher, and each time they make a grammatical change in the sentence according to the teacher's instructions[6]. In each new sentence, they must make the same kind of transformation. The sentence structure may vary or remain as it is: the essential thing is that the transformation should operate on the same grammatical point.

Example. Drill on sequence of tenses in indirect speech.

MODEL:	*Je demande où est Jean.*	I'm asking where John is.
	J'ai demandé où était Jean.	I was asking where John was.
Then:	*On me dit qu'il est absent.*	They tell me he's away.

On m'a dit qu'il était absent.	They told me he was away.
Je demande s'il voyage.	I ask if he's on a trip.
J'ai demandé s'il voyageait.	I asked if he was on a trip.
On me dit qu'il va partir.	They tell me he's going to leave.
On m'a dit qu'il allait partir.	They told me he was going to leave.

Aim. The transformation drill is based on the essential principle of opposition. Each drill brings into play one of the grammatical oppositions that are a feature of the language being learnt. In this case, the lexical content of the drill is ancillary. It would be possible to make up a transformation drill on the basis of nonsense sentences in which the only identifiable features would be the morphemes affected by the transformation. But the drill is naturally more interesting if the grammatical opposition is underlined by an obvious change in the meaning. Here again it is important to use lexical items that are already known, so that the learner can use them in a wider sense through the grammatical oppositions he is now mastering. On the other hand, transformation drill can be applied in the learning of purely lexical, rather than grammatical oppositions, as in the following examples:

| *Il fume souvent. C'est un fumeur.* | He often smokes. He's a smoker. |
| *Il ment souvent. C'est un menteur.* | He often tells lies. He's a liar. |

Comment. As there is an enormous variety of grammatical and lexical oppositions in any language, there will naturally be a very wide variety of possible transformation drills. Here are a few of the transformation drills that can be used for French and English:

(a) For the change from singular to plural, and *vice versa*:

| *J'ai un ami/J'ai des amis.* | I have a friend/I have some friends. |
| *Nous allons au ciméma/Je vais au cinéma.* | We're going to the cinema/ I'm going to the cinema. |

(b) For changes in tense:
>   *Il prend une glace/Il a pris*   He's taking an ice/He's
>   *une glace.*   taken an ice.

(c) For changes from affirmative to negative:
>   *Je parle français/Je ne parle*   I speak French/I don't speak
>   *pas français.*   French.

(d) For changes from affirmative to interrogative:
>   *Vous faites une promenade/*   You're going for a walk/
>   *Faites-vous une*   Are you going for a
>   *promenade?*   walk?

Variations. Transformation can operate by the replacement of one segment by another and at the same time by the displacement of one of the frames. This is not a case of substitution: the change remains the same throughout the drill and involves two opposing structures. The transformation affects not only certain morphemes but also their position in the sentence.

Example: Opposition: noun/pronoun.

>   *Je cherche mes livres/Je les*   I'm looking for my books/
>   *cherche.*   I'm looking for them.
>   *Je vais au musée/J'y vais.*   I'm going to the museum/
>   I'm going there.
>
>   *Je bois du lait/J'en bois.*   I'm drinking some milk/
>   I'm drinking some.

[In this example, *'displacement* of one of the frames' applies to French but not to English. There would be such displacement in English in the following example: I'm putting away my books/ I'm putting them away.]

In French, this is a very important drill, which can be applied to a great number of grammatical oppositions. Here is an example at a more advanced level:

>   *Je pense à ma mère/Je pense*   I'm thinking of my mother/
>   *à elle.*   I'm thinking of her:
>   *J'écris à ma mère/Je lui écris.*   I'm writing to my mother/
>   I'm writing to her.
>
>   *Je pense à mon examen/*   I'm thinking of my exam/
>   *J'y pense.*   I'm thinking of it.

EXPANSION

Form. The teacher suggests a series of segments that are to be introduced progressively into the structure of a basic sentence. Thus the sentence grows longer and longer as the pupils insert the new segments. This drill follows on naturally from the 'Substitution by expansion' exercise described earlier.

Example: Let us look back at the example given under 'Substitution by expansion.' This time, however, instead of giving the pupils the whole noun phrase, or adverb phrase as the case may be, the teacher will give only one segment of it, without indicating which phrase it belongs to. Thus:

Il est arrivé hier. (soir)	He arrived yesterday. (evening)
Il est arrivé hier soir. (Le garçon)	He arrived yesterday evening. (The boy)
Le garçon est arrivé hier soir. (jeune)	The boy arrived yesterday evening. (young)
Le jeune garçon est arrivé hier soir. (à neuf heures)	The young boy arrived yesterday evening. (at nine o'clock)
Le jeune garçon est arrivé hier soir à neuf heures. (blond)	The young boy arrived yesterday evening at nine o'clock. (fair)
Le jeune garçon blond est arrivé hier soir à neuf heures. (bien)	The fair young boy arrived yesterday evening at nine o'clock. (well or safely)
Le jeune garçon blond est bien arrivé hier soir à neuf heures. (qui parle)	The fair young boy arrived safely yesterday evening at nine o'clock. (who is speaking)
Le jeune garçon blond qui parle est bien arrivé hier soir à neuf heures.	The fair young boy who is speaking arrived safely yesterday evening, etc.

Aim. As with the 'substitution by expansion' drill, the pupils learn to appreciate the possible variations on an utterance, within its upper and lower limits. In addition, they are now obliged to recognise automatically which frame in the structure each new segment should be allotted to.

Comment. One cannot be too careful, in constructing this kind of drill, to prevent any possible uncertainty as to how each new segment should be used. For example, if instead of *blond* I had suggested *anglais* (English), the pupils would have good cause to hesitate between *le jeune garçon anglais* and *le jeune Anglais*. If I had suggested *bien* after having introduced *qui parle*, they would have hesitated between *est bien arrivé* (arrived safely) and *qui parle bien* (who speaks well).

COMBINATION

Form. Two simple sentences, of which the lexical content is chosen in such a way that there is an obvious relation between them, are joined to form one complex sentence. The three types of structure (simple sentence 1 + simple sentence 2 = complex sentence 3) remain fixed throughout the drill. Only the lexical content changes.

Example.

MODEL:	*Un homme arrive. C'est mon père. L'homme qui arrive est mon père.*	A man is arriving. It's my father. The man who's arriving is my father.
Then:	*Un garçon achète les billets. C'est Jacques. Le garçon qui achète les billets est Jacques.*	A boy is buying the tickets. It's Jack. The boy (who's) buying the tickets is Jack.
	Une jeune fille sonne à la porte. C'est notre voisine. La jeune fille qui sonne à la porte est notre voisine.	A young girl is ringing our bell. She's our neighbour. The young girl (who's) ringing our bell is our neighbour.

Aim. This type of drill is invaluable, because it is the only kind that provides adequate practice in certain grammatical structures, in relative pronouns in particular. The transition from two simple independent sentences to one complex sentence in which the two former sentences are merged, enables the pupils to grasp the logical relationships between the different constituent parts and to express them in the only single structure possible in the circumstances. The mechanism of the structure thus produced can operate without risk of interference from the habits of the mother tongue. With the help of this drill, for example, the English-speaking student can learn to use *dont* (= of which, of whom, or whose) in a single sentence type, without the risk of slipping into one of the English structures that *of which, of whom* or *whose* would require.

Comment. This type of structural drill can equally well be used in practising the sequence of tenses in two related clauses.

Example:

> *Ce matin, il fait beau. Jacques fait une excursion.*
> This morning, the weather's fine. Jack is going on an excursion.
>
> *Ce matin, s'il faisait beau, Jacques ferait une excursion.*
> This morning, if the weather was fine, Jack would go on an excursion.
>
> *Demain, il fera beau. Jacques fera une excursion.*
> Tomorrow it will be fine. Jack will go on an excursion.
>
> *Demain, s'il fait beau, Jacques fera une excursion.*
> Tomorrow, if it is fine, Jack will go on an excursion.
>
> *Hier, il faisait beau. Jacques a fait une excursion.*
> Yesterday it was fine. Jack went on an excursion.
>
> *Hier, s'il avait fait beau, Jacques aurait fait une excursion.*
> Yesterday, if it had been fine, Jack would have gone on an excursion.

CONTROLLED DIALOGUE

In the drills we have described so far, the pupil has had to imitate sentences given to him by the teacher, but to modify them in a variety of ways. The 'controlled dialogue' drills still keep the pupil within a context and within a strictly-controlled range of structures. At the same time they lay the foundations for real conversational interchange. They are therefore more natural and more alive than the other structural drills.

1

CONTRADICTION

Form. This drill is a near relation to the transformation drill which produces a negative structure in opposition to an affirmative one, but it does so in dialogue form. The teacher provides a structure in the form of a declaration and the pupil contradicts the declaration in such a way as to express a contrary opinion. The contradiction can be negative as opposed to affirmative, or *vice versa*. It can be prefaced by a variety of exclamations like *"Moi, je . . ."* (Personally, I . . .), *"Non, non, . . ."* (No, no, . . .), *"Mais non . . ."* (Oh no . . .), *"Si, si, . . ."* (Yes . . .), *"Au contraire . . ."* (On the contrary . . .) according to the instructions for each drill.

Example. Drill on the following oppositions:

    (a) plain affirmative/plain negative;

    (b) affirmative with **still**/negative with **no longer, no more**;

    (c) affirmative with **sometimes**/negative with **never**.

(a) *Moi, je peux m'en occuper.*   /*Eh bien, moi, je ne peux pas m'en occuper.*
Personally, I can deal with it.   Well, personally, I can't deal with it.

(b) *Moi, je peux encore m'en occuper.*   /*Eh bien, moi je ne peux plus m'en occuper.*
. . . I can still deal with it.   . . . I can't deal with it any longer.

(c) *Moi, je peux quelquefois m'en occuper.*   /*Eh bien, moi, je ne peux jamais m'en occuper.*
. . . I can sometimes deal with it.   . . . I can never deal with it.

(a) *Vous n'avez pas faim?*   /*Si, si, j'ai faim.*
You're not hungry?   *Yes,* I *am* hungry.

(b) *Vous n'avez plus faim?*   /*Si, si, j'ai encore faim.*
You're not hungry any more?   *Yes,* I'm *still* hungry.

(c) *Vous n'avez jamais faim?*   /*Si, si, j'ai quelquefois faim.*
You're never hungry?   *Yes,* I'm hungry *some*times.

Aim. Perhaps all that need be said at this point is that contradiction plays such an important role in any conversation between two French people, that to teach pupils how to handle it is to teach them an aspect of French culture. Anyway, contradicting one's teacher is perhaps such a rare pleasure that one might as well enjoy it. However, contradiction drills have a more serious aim than that — namely to help the pupil master the various affirmative/negative and negative/affirmative oppositions in as real a context as possible, with the support of other indications of contradiction that normally occur in conversation, especially intonation.

Comment. It is worth remembering that, in French, certain affirmative/negative oppositions entail not only the addition or deletion of certain words but also morphological changes that may not occur in another language, e.g. English. *Moi, je sais qu'il reviendra/Moi, je ne sais pas s'il reviendra* (I know he'll come back/I don't know if he'll come back) presents no great problem for speakers of English. But the following types of opposition call for intensive training if interference by the pupil's mother tongue is to be overcome:

<table>
<tr><td>Moi, je suis sûr qu'il viendra
I'm sure he'll come.</td><td>/Moi, je ne suis pas sûr qu'il
    vienne.
I'm not sure that he'll come.</td></tr>
<tr><td>Vous avez de la patience
You do have patience.</td><td>/Mais non, je n'ai pas de
    patience.
Oh no, I've no patience.</td></tr>
<tr><td>Regardez-le
Look at him.</td><td>/Ne le regardez pas.
Don't look at him.</td></tr>
</table>

2

INJUNCTION

Form. The sentences given by the pupils in this drill form part of a dialogue, since they are all addressed to a definite person, whom the teacher indicates. The teacher also suggests the semantic content of the sentence. As for the structure that must be used, the pupil deduces this directly from what he has just been told, viz. address your remark to a certain person, and tell him the following. The teacher's instructions will therefore begin like this:

Dites à X que . . .	Tell X that . . .
Dites à X de . . .	Tell X to . . .
Demandez à X si . . .	Ask X if . . .
Demandez à X de . . .	Ask X to . . .

This drill can be carried out in two different ways. The teacher can either address each pupil in turn, telling him what to say and to whom it should be said (as in Example 1 opposite), or he

162

can choose two or three pupils, directing a conversation between them (as in Example 2).

Example (1) Drill on the imperative followed by a personal pronoun.

> *Dites à Paul de vous demander au téléphone, vous seul.*
> — *Paul, demandez-moi au téléphone.*

Tell Paul to ask for you on the 'phone.
— Paul, ask for me on the 'phone.

> *Dites à Paul de demander Jean au téléphone.*
> — *Paul, demandez-le au téléphone.*

Tell Paul to ask for John on the 'phone.
— Paul, ask for him on the 'phone.

> *Dites à Paul de demander Jean et Jeanne au téléphone.*
> — *Paul, demandez-les au téléphone.*

Tell Paul to ask for John and Jean on the 'phone.

— Paul, ask for them on the 'phone.

Example (2)

> *Demandez à Paul s'il veut aller au cinéma.*
> — *Paul, veux-tu aller au cinéma?*

Ask Paul if he wants to go to the cinema.
— Paul, do you want to go to the cinema?

> *Répondez-lui que vous regrettez, mais que vous êtes fatigué.*
> — *Je regrette, mais je suis fatigué.*

Tell him you're sorry, but you're tired.

— I'm sorry, but I'm tired.

> *Demandez-lui ce qu'il a fait hier.*
> — *Qu'est-ce que tu as fait hier?*

Ask him what he did yesterday.
— What did you do yesterday?

Aim. These injunction drills form an excellent bridge between the more mechanical assimilation exercises on the one hand and spontaneous conversation on the other. Although the injunction is so worded as to require a response of a certain grammatical kind, it is none the less up to the pupil to find the precisely appropriate structure. The pupil thus develops the habit of reacting to a certain stimulus, immediately extracting the necessary information and using it to formulate his response. The very necessity to extract this semantic information from what he hears, before making his response, avoids the danger, always latent in many structural drills, that the pupil may not understand, or may misunderstand, what he is saying. The injunction drills therefore provide an excellent means of making sure that structures which the pupils have already practised are not without their proper semantic content.

Comment. The degree of difficulty in this kind of drill varies with the form the injunction takes. *Dites à Henri que vous êtes malade* (Tell Henry you're ill) requires no more than two simple operations: extracting *vous êtes malade* (you're ill) from the injunction and transforming it into *je suis malade* (I'm ill). On the other hand, *Dites à Paul de ne pas vous rendre votre livre* (Tell Paul not to give you back your book) calls for a much more complicated series of operations: (1) over the purely referential frame (i.e. the idea of giving back a book to the speaker), the pupil has to superimpose several notions of a grammatical nature; viz. (2) an imperative, an order to the person who has to perform the action; (3) a negation of that order; (4) an indirect object, referring to the person to whom the book should not be given back; (5) a possessive adjective, referring to the person whose book it is. If the pupil is not already familiar with each of those operations taken separately, the drill will present practically insurmountable difficulties and will only lead to chaos. So it is essential that the teacher should always have a clear idea of what operations are demanded by an injunction drill and should know how to grade the difficulties.

3

QUESTION-AND-ANSWER

Form: We shall only be considering here question-and-answer exercises from a structural point of view, that is to say when the question obliges the pupil to use a certain grammatical structure which the teacher has chosen as object of the lesson. Most transformation drills, of the kind described above, can be done by question and answer, and that gives them a more natural direction, leading the pupil to the threshold of normal conversation. Contradiction drills also lend themselves well to question and answer, e.g. *Vous ne croyez pas qu'il vienne? Si, si, je crois qu'il viendra* (You don't think he'll come? Oh yes, I think he *will* come). If the grammatical structure required in the answer is a complex one, it is better to keep variations in the lexis to a minimum so that the pupil's attention can be focused on the grammatical transformation. On the other hand, if the object of the exercise is to practise using certain lexical items, then the grammatical structure should be varied as little as possible. In any case, the pupil should be given a model answer before he starts doing the drill on his own.

Example. Drill on personal pronouns, as direct and indirect objects.

MODEL: *Est-ce que tu as donné à Jean les objets qui sont arrivés pour lui?*
Have you given John the things that came for him?

Ah non, tiens! j'ai oublié de les lui donner.
No, there now, I forgot to give them to him.

Est-ce que tu as remis à Jean les objets qui sont arrivés pour lui?
Have you given John back the things that came for him?

Ah non, tiens, j'ai oublié de les lui remettre.
No, there now, I forgot to give them back to him.

Est-ce que tu as donné à Jeanne les bagages qui sont arrivés pour elle?
Have you given Jean the luggage that came for her?

Ah non, tiens, j'ai oublié de les lui donner.
No, there now, I forgot to give them to her.

Aim. Question-and-answer exercises, which have always been part of the standard practice of language classes, are designed to 'make the pupil speak' and to activate the vocabulary and grammar that he has learnt in the course of his reading and his study of the rules. In audio-lingual methods, lexis and syntax are activated orally from the very beginning, so that, as far as activation is concerned, question-and-answer no longer holds a privileged place. Nevertheless, like the other controlled-dialogue exercises described in this article, question-and-answer gives the pupil the opportunity of reacting automatically to certain syntactical situations and of exercising some degree of personal choice in the forms he selects: he can thus begin to react as someone who really speaks and thinks, rather than as an automaton mechanically controlled. A question like 'What did you do yesterday?' is right outside the area of structural drills, since the person to whom it is addressed is left entirely free to choose the syntactical and lexical content of his reply. He could not, however, make successful use of this freedom had he not been led systematically and progressively to the point at which he could give well-formed answers as a matter of habit and without having to think consciously of the linguistic problems latent in his reply. The aim of question-and-answer is therefore to overcome the final obstacle in the way of freedom of expression.

Variation. Statement-Question-Answer

By combining transformation, substitution and question-and-answer, one can construct a drill that provides an opportunity for dialogue between one pupil and another, rather than the orthodox exchange between teacher and learner. Instead of asking the pupils a question to which they must reply, the teacher makes a statement, affirmative or negative. One of the pupils puts this statement into the interrogative (by transformation), changing the subject (by substitution) in the process. His neighbour then replies to the question, in the question-and-answer situation.

Example:

M R P: I gave back your photographs to John this morning.

1st PUPIL: Did Mr P. give back your photographs to John this morning?

2nd PUPIL: Oh yes, he gave them back to him.

An exercise of this kind has the advantage of allowing the pupils themselves to ask the questions: this role is too often regarded as being the teacher's exclusively. Like the injunction drill, it makes an excellent starting point for spontaneous conversation. There is no objection to leaving the first pupil free to replace the subject of the original sentence by whatever noun or noun phrase he likes. Indeed, both pupils should ultimately be free to make substitutions in other frames as well, e.g. in the verb, direct object or indirect object. Note, however, that such an exercise can only be done in the classroom: it is not suitable for the language laboratory.

COMPLETION

Form. The traditional exercise requiring pupils to complete sentences of which certain segments have been replaced by dashes or blanks is essentially a *written* exercise. It can hardly be done orally: it could produce ridiculous utterances punctuated by 'blank, blank'. However, when certain structures have been thoroughly practised with the help of drills of different kinds, pupils can profitably be required to do, in class, a completion exercise in which the teacher gives them the first part of a sentence, leaving them to supply the rest. However, in such a case the second part of the sentence must be closely linked, structurally, with the first part. This exercise is particularly useful in mastering the sequence of tenses. The pupil should have a degree of freedom of expression. He can exercise his imagination in the choice of lexis. We have reached, in other words, the extreme limit of structural drill.

Examples. Sentences of which only the first part is given.

    If I was hungry, I . . . .
    As I was thirsty, I . . . .
    As soon as I had understood, I . . . .
    While I was telephoning, I . . . .

[The final paragraph of Madame Delattre's article has already been quoted by Monsieur Girard, particularly on page 69.]

NOTES AND BIBLIOGRAPHICAL REFERENCES

Introduction

1. See note 20 on Chapter One. This quotation comes from *Principles of Language Study*, 1921, and was used by Donn Byrne in *English Teaching Extracts* (Longman).

Author's Preface

1. WILLIAM FRANCIS MACKEY, Director of the International Center for Research in Bilingualism, Laval University, Quebec. His *Language Teaching Analysis* (Longman), was first published in 1965.

Chapter One

1. GASTON BERGER (1896-1960), creator of *la prospective*, the scientific study of the future, and a famous Director of Higher Education in France, who insisted on the importance of continual re-training.

2. COMENIUS was the Latinized name of Johann Amos Comensky, of Moravia, Czechoslovakia. He published his *Ianua linguarum reserata* (The Gate of Languages Unlocked) in 1631, and his *Orbus pictus*, the first known book to teach language through pictures, in 1658.

3. FRANÇOIS GOUIN, *The Art of Teaching and Studying Languages*, was translated by H. Swan and V. Bétis and published in London, 1894. There is a fuller reference to Gouin in Chapter Three, p. 35.

4. FERDINAND DE SAUSSURE'S *Cours de Linguistique Générale* was translated into English by Wade Baskin under the title *Course in General Linguistics* (Philosophical Library, New York, 1959).

5. NOAM CHOMSKY, Professor of Modern Languages and Linguistics at the Massachusetts Institute of Technology, U.S.A., has written *Syntactic Structures* (1957), a critical review of B. F. Skinner's *Verbal Behavior* (1959), *Aspects of the Theory of Syntax* (1965), *Cartesian Linguistics* (1966), etc.

6. This work, by the teachers at the Port-Royal monastery in Paris and published under the title *Grammaire générale et raisonnée* in 1660, aimed to demonstrate that the structure of language is a product of reason.

7. The author discusses the notion of structure and its practical application to language teaching, in Chapter Four. While the terms 'structure', 'structural', etc. are widely used in linguistics and language teaching, they have different meanings and associations; and the term 'structuralist' has been the source of controversy referred to by Denis Girard himself (see General Introduction, page ix). A useful reference to the objection to one 'set of assumptions' associated with structural linguistics will be found in the *Introduction to Theoretical Linguistics* by John Lyons (Cambridge University Press, 1968). This does not seem to invalidate the case for the practical application of the notion of structure to language teaching, as put forward by the author in Chapter Four.

8. BERTIL MALMBERG, *Les nouvelles tendances de la linguistique,* 1966 (translated from the Swedish publication of 1962): this work was translated into English by E. Carney, as *New trends in linguistics,* Stockholm, 1964.

9. The 'synchronic method' is explained on pages 5-6. Its importance for language teachers lies in its·appeal to *what is said and what is acceptable today* as a criterion for what is 'correct', rather than an appeal to the history of the language.

10. 'Descriptive' may be contrasted with 'prescriptive', which refers to dogmatic assertions about what *should* be said.

11. EDWARD SAPIR, *Language: An Introduction to the Study of Speech* (New York, Harcourt, Bruce and World, 1921).

12. LEONARD BLOOMFIELD, *Language* (New York, Holt, Rinehart and Winston, 1933; and London, Allen and Unwin, 1935).

13. See Bloomfield's *Outline Guide for the Practical Study of Foreign Languages,* published by the Linguistics Society of America, Waverly Press, Baltimore, 1942.

14. ANDRÉ MARTINET, *Eléments de Linguistique Générale* (Paris, Armand Colin, 1960), translated into English by Elizabeth Palmer, under the title *Elements of General Linguistics* (London, Faber and Faber, 1964).

15. "I am, frankly, rather skeptical about the significance, for the teaching of languages, of such insights and understanding as have been attained in linguistics and psychology." (N. CHOMSKY, *Linguistic Theory,* Northeast Conference on *Research and Language Learning,* 1966).

16. W. VIËTOR, *Der Sprachunterricht muss umkehren* (Leipzig, 1902).

17. ABBÉ J-P. ROUSSELOT (1846-1924), author of *Précis de prononciation française* (1902), a pioneer in experimental phonetics and the first language teaching expert known to have recommended the use, for teaching purposes, of recorded sound (by means of the phonograph).

18. PAUL PASSY: see, for example, his *De la méthode directe dans l'enseignement des langues vivantes,* 1899; and *La phonétique et ses applications* (London, International Phonetic Association, 1929).

19. DANIEL JONES, *An Outline of English Phonetics* (W. Heffer, first published 1918, several editions since), *Everyman's English Pronouncing Dictionary* (London, Dent, first published 1917; 13th edition edited by A. C. Gimson, 1967, also published in New York by E. P. Dutton); etc.

20. H. E. PALMER was Director of the Institute for Research in Language Teaching, Tokyo, author of *The Oral Method of Teaching Languages* (Heffer, 1923), *A Grammar of Spoken English* (Heffer, 1924, and twice revised), *A Grammar of English Words* (Longman, 1938), etc. His first work, *The Scientific Study and Teaching of Languages* (1917), is very relevant to Monsieur Girard's general thesis.

21. J. R. FIRTH, Professor of General Linguistics, London University, 1944-1957. See *In Memory of J. R. Firth* (Longman, 1966) which gives not only an account of his work but also an indication of his influence.

22. C. C. FRIES, was Director of the English Language Institute at Ann Arbor, Michigan, and exerted a world-wide influence in the 1940's and 1950's. See *The Teaching of English* (Ann Arbor: Wahr, 1949) and *The Structure of English* (New York, Harcourt, 1952; London, Longman, 1957), etc.

23. PIERRE DELATTRE, was at the University of California, Santa Barbara. See particularly his *Studies in French and Comparative Phonetics* (The Hague, Mouton, 1966).

24. Perhaps the best known example is that of Paul Roberts who accepted Chomsky's ideas on transformation in grammar and applied them in *Modern Grammar* (Harcourt, Brace and World, 1967-1968).

25. See Author's Preface, Note 1.

26. ARCHIBALD A. HILL, *Introduction to Linguistic Structures* (New York, Harcourt, 1958), etc.

27. Z. S. HARRIS, *Structural Linguistics* (University of Chicago Press, 1961), *Transformational Theory* (1965), etc.

28. VIGGO BRØNDAL, *The Parts of Speech* (Copenhagen, 1928), translated into French, 1948.

29. KENNETH L. PIKE, *Language in Relation to a Unified Theory of Human Behavior* (revised edition, The Hague, Mouton, 1967). R. H. Robins defines a tagmeme as 'a place in a structure (syntactic or morphological) together with a formal class of elements occupying that place (often referred to as a 'slot' with its 'filler')' (*General Linguistics: An Introductory Survey*, 2nd Edition, Longman, 1971).

30. R. E. LONGACRE, *Some fundamental insights of tagmemics*, in the journal *Language*, Baltimore, 1965.

31. The term 'immediate constituents', now widely used in linguistics, was introduced by Bloomfield, and could be defined, simply, as 'the parts of a sentence that follow one another in such a way as to make the sentence grammatical'. For a very helpful description, see John Lyons's *Introduction to Theoretical Linguistics*, section 6.1.2.

32. The theories of transformational grammar are associated with the name of Z. S. Harris (see note 27), and particularly with that of Noam Chomsky (note 5) who refers more specifically to 'transformational-generative grammar'.

33. JEAN PIAGET, *Le langage et la pensée chez l'enfant* (Neuchâtel, Switzerland, 1923), translated by M. Gabain under the title of *The Language and Thought of the Child* (London: Routledge and Kegan Paul, 1932).

34. ROBERT LADO, collaborated with C. C. Fries at Ann Arbor (see note 22), also author of *Linguistics across Cultures* (Ann Arbor, 1957), *Language Testing* (London, 1961). He later became Academic Director of the Institute of Languages and Linguistics, Georgetown University.

Chapter Two

1. M. A. K. HALLIDAY, ANGUS McINTOSH and PETER STREVENS, *The Linguistic Sciences and Language Teaching* (Longman, 1964).

2. *English Language Teaching* (journal published by the Oxford University Press in association with the British Council), Vol. 17, No. 2, January 1963.

3. See Chapter One, note 14.

4. S. PIT CORDER, Head of the Department of Applied Linguistics, University of Edinburgh, *The Visual Element in Language Teaching* (Longman, 1966).

5. See R. LADO, *Linguistics across Cultures,* Chapter One, note 34, particularly the reference to the different connotations of the word 'bullfight' for English-speakers and Spanish-speakers.

Chapter Three

1. See particularly LEO L. KELLY, *Dialogue versus Structural Approach,* in *The French Review,* February 1964; F. L. MARTY, introduction to *Action French: Dialogue,* Audio-Visual Publications, 1964; and LÉOPOLD TAILLON, *Présentation dialoguée versus enseignement structural,* paper read to the Canadian Association of Linguistics, 1964.

2. SIEUR DU TERTRE, *Méthode générale et raisonnée pour apprendre facilement les langues,* Paris, 1651.

3. COLLOT, *Progressive French Dialogues and Phrases,* 1873.

4. See Chapter One, notes 22 and 34. In a more recent work, *Language Teaching,* Robert Lado comes down in favour of dialogue, on the grounds that it facilitates dramatisation and provides a motive from the start.

5. PIERRE DELATTRE, *Une technique audio-linguale,* article in *Le Français dans le Monde,* December 1962. See Chapter One, note 23.

6. C.R.E.D.I.F. = *Centre de Recherche et d'Etude pour la Diffusion du Français,* at Saint-Cloud, near Paris.

7. The Audio-Visual Centre at Saint-Cloud was a pioneer in audio-visual methods of language teaching.

8. The University of Zagreb, Yugoslavia, has also been a pioneer in modern methods of language teaching thanks particularly to Professor R. FILIPOVIČ (English) and Professor P. GUBERINA (Phonetics).

9. See the previous note.

10. *Voix et Images de France,* produced by C.R.E.D.I.F. (see note 6 above) and published by Didier, 1962.

11. *Pierre et Seydou,* a French course produced by B.E.L.C. for English-speaking pupils in Africa and published by Hachette.

12. An example of the redundant features in written French is given in Chapter Five.

13. The terms in inverted commas in this sentence are used in transformational-generative grammar.

14. A method of learning by which the student can check his own results: if he is right, he can proceed to the next stage; if he is wrong, he is obliged to repeat the previous step until he finds the right answer.

Chapter Four

1. *Notions de structure et structure de la connaissance* (Paris, A. Michel, 1957).

2. LUCIEN TESNIÈRE, *Eléments de syntaxe structurale* (Paris, Klinsksieck, revised, 1965).

3. J. MAROUZEAU, *Lexique de la terminologie linguistique* (Paris, Geuthner, 1951).

4. R. BASTIDE, *Sens et usage du terme structure* (The Hague, Mouton, 1962).

5. L. HJELMSLEV, *Structural Linguistics,* in the journal of the Linguistic Circle of Copenhagen, Vol. XII, 1959.

6. See NOAM CHOMSKY, *Aspects of the Theory of Syntax,* 1965.

7. A. JUILLAND, *Structural Relations* (The Hague, Mouton, 1961).

8. See note 2.

9. For a detailed study on this subject, *De la Linguistique à la pédagogie: le verbe français,* by M. CSECSY (Paris, Hachette-Larousse, 1968).

10. See P. LÉON, *Laboratoires de langues et correction phoné-tique* (Paris, Didier, 1962).

11. F. W. GRAVIT and A. VALDMAN, *Report of the Third Language Laboratory Conference,* also published by Mouton, The Hague, 1963.

12.   Exercises on the French possessives and *Il faut,* with tapes, B.E.L.C.

13.   F.   RÉQUÉDAT,   *Les   exercices   structuraux*   (Paris, Hachette-Larousse, 1966).

14.   P. DELATTRE, *La notion de structure et son utilité* in *Le Français dans le Monde,* No. 41, June 1966.

15.   M.   LÉON,   *Exercices systématiques de prononciation française* (Paris, Hachette-Larousse, 1964).

16.   D. HUGONNET, *Exercices de français pour le laboratoire de langues,* with tapes (Paris, Cédamel, 1966).

17.   A. GAUTHIER, *My friend Tony,* with tapes (Paris, Didier, 1966).

18.   *Op. cit.,* note 14.

19.   B. F. SKINNER'S *Verbal Behavior* (New York, Appleton Century Crofts, 1957) was the subject of a critical review by Chomsky: see Chapter One, note 5. This is a case where, as Girard himself has pointed out, the truth may well lie between two extremes. In any case, the four-phase drills described by Skinner have been, and are still being, used with success in a great many language laboratories.

20.   This is an example of the influence of K. L. Pike's 'tagmemic' theory: see Chapter One, note 29.

21.   An example of the application of transformational-generative grammar.

22.   See appendix.

23.   In Chapter Six, the author explains exactly how a lesson can be planned and conducted along these lines.

24.   See note 13.

Chapter Five

1. See Lado's *Linguistics across Cultures* (Chapter One, note 34).

2. See E. WAGNER, *Passage de la langue commune à la langue littéraire,* published by Hachette-Larousse for B.E.L.C.

3. See C. STOURDZÉ, *La reconstitution de texte,* article in *Le Français dans le Monde,* No. 17, June 1963.

Chapter Six

1. A complete list of these exercises appears in F. RÉQUÉDAT'S book referred to in Chapter Four, note 13.

2. See the article by A. GAUTHIER in *Le Français dans le Monde,* No. 19, pp. 15-17; also Chapter Four, note 17.

Chapter Seven

1. *The Teaching of Modern Language* (UNESCO Seminar, Ceylon, August 1953, Chapter VI).

2. See R. LADO, *Language Teaching: A Scientific Approach* (Boston, McGraw Hill, 1964).

3. See the circular issued by the Council of Europe on the 'Meeting of experts on the training and further training of modern language teachers' (Paris, March 1964).

4. JEAN ONIMUS, *L'Enseignement des Lettres et la Vie* (Desclée de Brower, 1965).

5. Resolution No. 2 of the Conference of European Ministers of Education (Rome, October 1962).

Chapter Eight

1. See note 1 on Author's Preface.

2. *Language Teaching Analysis,* page 3.

3. *Op. cit.* Chapter Two, note 1.

4. W. F. MACKEY and J. G. SAVARD, *The Indices of Coverage,* article in *The International Review of Applied Linguistics* (Heidelberg), Vol. V/2-3, 1967.

5. M. G. NEWMARK, *A Field Test of Three Approaches to the Teaching of Spanish in Elementary Schools* (California State Department of Education, Sacramento, 1966).

6. Reference is made here to an unpublished article by Mackey entitled *Practice Teaching: Models and Modules.*

Appendix

1. NELSON BROOKS, *Language and Language Learning,* 2nd Edition, New York, Harcourt Brace, 1964.

2. ROBERT LADO, *Language Teaching,* New York, McGraw-Hill, 1964.

3. ROBERT POLITZER, *Teaching French: An Introduction to Applied Linguistics*, Boston, Ginn and Co., 1960.

4. Madame Delattre uses the term 'opposition' to refer to changes on the paradigmatic axis.

5. Examples of this redundancy are, in English, *The books are . . .*, and, in French, *Les livres sont. . . .* In both of those examples the idea of plurality is expressed more than once.

6. Madame Delattre makes it clear in the notes on her article that she considers the teacher is better advised to give good models illustrating a grammatical point than to attempt an abstract explanation.